# CONTENTS

# INTRODUCTION

In November 1987 the 'Design Matters' series presented four new programmes about the role of designers in shaping the future of our cities. Each programme looked in detail at a particular place – Belfast, Glasgow, Newcastle and Southampton – and asked: what kind of place will it be by the year 2000? What will people be doing there? What products will they be making? What kinds of houses will they live in? Where will they shop? What will they buy? What will they do in their spare time? Will their surroundings have improved or declined? Do we in fact have a clear idea of what the future should be like? If we do, have we the skill and resources to bring it into existence?

The design of places and products cannot be separated when discussing the future of cities. Cities exist for a purpose. The purpose may vary, but every city needs a firm economic foundation if it is to flourish and be a pleasant place in which to live. Places that are good to be in will attract new enterprise and people with entrepreneurial drive. The wealth-creating power of product development is one of the engines needed to drive urban improvement, but the quality and responsiveness of the townscape is itself an important factor in attracting new business and energetic people.

Newcastle City Libraries

*Cover of an issue of* British Workman *for January 1859 celebrating the career of George Stephenson. It was on the inventiveness of engineering designers like Stephenson that the early prosperity of Britain's industrial cities depended.*

Newcastle City Libraries

*Dean Street, Newcastle, in 1870. The streets of 19th-century cities were full of life and bustle. Civil engineers designed splendid new structures, and municipal services – sewage disposal, clean water, street lighting – began to develop. All this activity depended on the wealth created by designing and making products for markets world wide.*

The Press Association

*Even in the 19th century there were periods of recession. But in the 1900s Britain began to lose her industrial supremacy. This was masked by the frenetic manufacturing activity associated with two world wars, but in the 1930s and again in the 1970s and 1980s the results were massive unemployment, social unrest and a declining physical environment. The Jarrow Crusade of 1936, sadly, was repeated fifty years later.*

The future of cities is a political issue. The parties compete with each other in putting forward proposals to solve urban problems and, following the 1987 General Election, the Government has put the inner cities at the top of its agenda. The 'Design Matters' programmes, however, were not primarily concerned with the struggle over resources or the battle between central and local government. They asked whether or not we now have effective design ideas to match resources – wherever they come from. After years of industrial decline, can we develop new products that will compete in world markets? Do we know how to turn the worst buildings of the 1960s and 1970s into places that are convenient, good looking and safe? Have we the design skills to capitalise on the economic shift from heavy industry into the leisure, fashion and service areas? Do we have the right design principles for the future?

The process of decline is well documented. There has been very much less investigation of the design elements needed to create an upward spiral. The programmes focused on places where regeneration is taking place, and asked what has made it a success. Do these developments have features in common? Could the approaches be made to work in other places? Are there implications for future policy? How can the local community, industry, engineers, designers, architects and planners get their act together?

*The late 1980s and 1990s will be a testing time for Britain's old manufacturing cities. They have to re-invent a role for themselves. No longer can they rely on wealth from the old heavy engineering technologies. They have to design products that people will want to buy in the future. And there is every sign that city-dwellers will no longer tolerate the legacy of bad design from the past. Two examples from Tyneside offer a glimpse of future directions. The Byker Estate – built a decade ago – demonstrates many of the human qualities now being designed into new and refurbished housing, and the Cryptag electronic decoder, developed at the Innovation Centre, symbolises the crucial importance of new technologies like microelectronics and biomedical engineering.*

Charles Mapleston

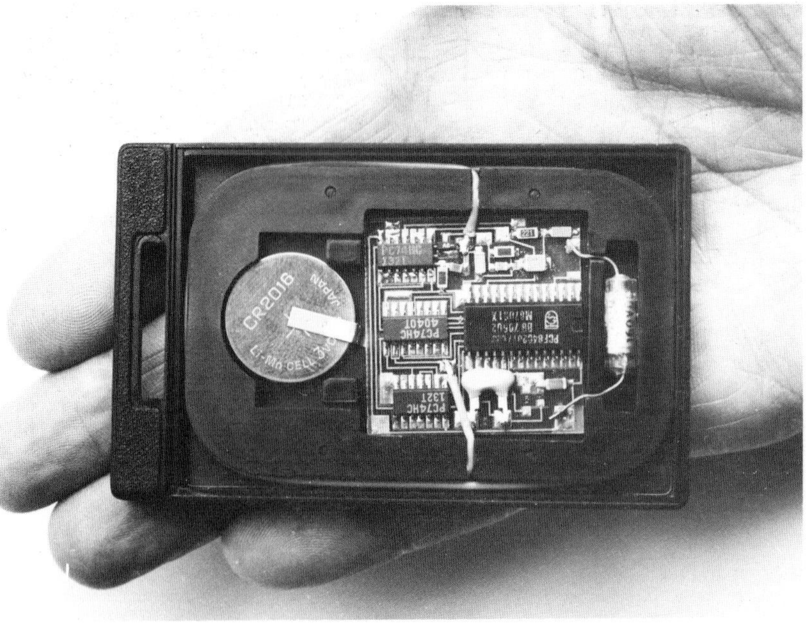


Charles Mapleston

The need to find answers to these questions is urgent. In the next decade there will be a series of industrial opportunities related to world markets that we may, or may not, take. In the same way, the decay of the environment will, at a certain point, be impossible to stop. There is, in fact, a small window of opportunity, after which much housing will be beyond repair and industrial prowess damaged beyond recovery.

These are not issues that can be left entirely to experts. The community needs to have a voice. But it needs more than a voice. Very effective action is being taken by ordinary people who are concerned about the future of their environment. It is now recognised that listening to what people want, and making use of the detailed local knowledge of residents, actually leads to better design. Another encouraging development is the growing economic importance of small businesses. In many cases these are led by people who are close to their market and who have particular insights into design and technology. Other people need to be helped to take similar independent initiatives.

This book is intended to help in two ways: first by giving examples of what has been done, and second by setting out some of the sources of help that are available.

# HAVE CITIES A FUTURE?

Cities have always been a focus for anxiety. Moralists, philosophers, economists, architects and politicians have all been concerned by the explosive growth of cities and the resulting urban problems. Planning laws for London date from the 15th century, while Vitruvius, the Roman architect/engineer, castigated the overcrowding and bad living conditions in the tenement blocks of his day. Everywhere the uncontrolled development of cities seems to have given rise to slums, crime and, frequently, political unrest. But this has not stopped urban growth, nor has it stopped people flocking to live in urban centres. Whatever their faults, cities are centres of economic power and places of opportunity and specialisation where many different skills and life styles can co-exist. Cities have also inspired imaginative design. The search for an urban ideal, better conditions and a more human environment, has existed alongside the problems. The results can be seen in every large city in Britain, often cheek by jowl with buildings that are the meanest expression of greed and economic exploitation. Elegant squares and crescents, spacious parks, great hospitals, railway stations like cathedrals, art galleries and museums, broad shopping streets and huge central markets testify not only to the great wealth of these cities in their prime but also to their social idealism and community spirit. Planning of this breadth and sweep is typical of cities: it gives them their sense of scale and excitement.

Specialists have laboured intensively over the years since the Industrial Revolution to untie the knot of poverty, overcrowding, dilapidation and poor environment. Success has been hard to achieve. After the Second World War, a powerful determination existed to eradicate poor housing and to create new communities where such problems would be a thing of the past. The social planners had great skill and resources at their disposal. Yet, in 1987, poor housing, like unemployment, remains a common social evil. In Glasgow, for example, 15 per cent of the housing stock is 'below tolerable standard' and 43 per cent of all dwellings needed over £3000 spent on them in 1985. Within these two categories, 13 per cent and 45 per cent respectively of the dwellings actually belong to the Glasgow District Council itself! Bailie Jim McLean, convenor of the Housing Committee, told the 1986 Inquiry into Housing in Glasgow, that 'we . . . know that we are on the threshold of the worst housing crisis this century'. Liverpool, London, Manchester and Birmingham share this awareness with Glasgow.

The Mitchell Library

*Slum tenements in the Gorbals, Glasgow.*

Every city has its fine houses and its few fashionable streets but the average town or suburban house or flat does not reach a high standard of functional or visual design. We do not visit the residential streets of our own period in search of pleasing buildings: for that we have to seek out the past, looking at Georgian

The Mitchell Library

*Glasgow's fine municipal centre at George Square.*

terraces in Newcastle or Brighton, the fine warehouses of Glasgow's Merchant City, or the unique Victorian suburb of Nottingham's Park Estate.

Cities are experiencing a withering economic blizzard, brought about first by the oil crisis of 1973-74 and then by the great strides made during the progress of new technology and the concomitant collapse of traditional manufacturing industry. Even a city like Southampton, in the apparently comfortable South East, has had to face up to an extraordinary change in its employment pattern. Although the city's docks still handle as much goods traffic as ever, mechanisation, containerisation and an increase in the size of ships, means that 650 dockers now do the work that 2800 did in 1974. The change is not only measured in employment terms. Containerisation has made the oldest docks, just where they join on to the city centre, obsolete. What will this space be used for? How can it provide work and prosperity?

On Clydeside, the collapse of shipbuilding and engineering is more dramatic. At Clydebank alone, the closure of the Singer factory and a large part of the John Brown shipyard resulted in the loss of 5000 jobs, and left acres of derelict land. To the east of Glasgow city centre the Scottish Development Agency is co-ordinating contributions from central and local government and private investors to rejuvenate an area covering 4000 acres (1618 ha), a large amount of it on land abandoned by industry. The project is known as GEAR (Glasgow Eastern Area Renewal), and is aimed directly at a part of the city where every social indicator of economic distress – employment, health, housing – is well below average.

The decision-makers in our cities have not been quick to grasp and plan for the underlying changes in the world economy and, in particular, the growth of the leisure industry and service sector. This may be partly because London has traditionally played a dominant role in finance and services while leisure has been associated with more visibly historic cities like Bath, York, Edinburgh, and the seaside resorts. However, the shift of emphasis is not new. Writing in *The Economy of Cities* as long ago as 1969, Jane Jacobs said 'Manufacturing work will, I think, no longer be the chief activity around which other economic activities are organised, as it is today and as the work of merchants once was. Instead, services will become the predominant organisational work, the instigators of other economic activities, including manufacturing.'

The combination of continuing, unsolved social and environmental problems with changes in technology, markets and employment is nothing less than revolutionary. The majority of our large cities result from and relate to forms and ideas that came about in the 19th century. The last two decades have seen those forms and ideas become largely irrelevant. To succeed in the 21st century, Britain's cities must re-invent themselves. They have to find new functions if they are to continue to flourish.

Fortunately, cities thrive on change. They have massive human and material resources. What they also need, however, is a sense of direction. In the immediate past this has been hard to find. The tremendous pressures of economic and environmental decline produced at first a defensive reaction; a resistance to change and an inclination to see the future in terms of images from the past. This is no longer the case. Routes to survival are being surveyed and new possibilities are being explored. Glasgow, whose environment had reached rock bottom in the early 1970s, saw a new and optimistic picture of itself in the Lord Provost's 'Miles Better'

*Glasgow still has slums – dereliction and abandonment at Easterhouse in 1987.*

Charles Mapleston

Charles Mapleston

*Glasgow University rises above the leafy streets in the west of the city. The contrast with Easterhouse is dramatic and painful.*

Charles Mapleston

*Acres of abandoned industrial land adjoin Glasgow's city centre. These areas in East Glasgow share the burden of excessive unemployment, bad housing and complex social deprivation.*

campaign. Now, with the Burrell Collection open, the Scottish Exhibition Centre thriving, the Garden Festival scheduled for 1988 and the prospect of becoming cultural capital of Europe in 1990, the silence of the Clydeside shipyards is easier to bear. In a similar way, Southampton has pieced together a viable shape for the future by emphasising its historical heritage, opening up land towards the sea, encouraging new shopping centres and the growth of new, advanced technology industries.

Each of the four cities featured here is in the process of re-inventing a unique role for itself. To do this means making use of its particular geography, the skills of its people, world market opportunities and the resources of its inherited buildings and places. We examine these unique plans for the future in the sections on each of the cities. But there are also a number of common elements. The next three sections identify these and spell out their significance for designers and planners.

# MANUFACTURE, EMPLOYMENT AND THE NEW ENVIRONMENT

A massive shift is taking place in our economy from manufacturing to service and leisure industries. This is not peculiar to the United Kingdom: it is happening all over the developed world. It is the result of a complex of technological changes, all of which lead in the same direction – to greater productivity. Less plant and fewer people are needed to produce more material, energy, products and transportation. And, as a result of good engineering design, the products themselves are also very much more productive and long lasting. The effect is exponential.

Shipbuilding provides one example. Ships have grown larger while their crews have grown smaller because of containerisation, mechanisation and automation. They spend only a short time in port because of the speed of the machinery used to unload them, but they also call at fewer, larger ports. A few big ships now do the work of many smaller ships, but modern computer-aided design and manufacturing techniques and the use of unit construction systems also means that each is quicker to design and build and needs many fewer people to construct it.

In all heavy industry, technology and good design tend towards:

- more automation and less employment
- the development of larger and more productive units
- equipment that makes efficient use of scarce and/or expensive resources in energy, space, materials and people.

Exactly the same trends can be seen in the production of consumer goods.

It is not surprising, therefore, that the United Kingdom has lost a huge amount of employment in traditional industries. However brilliant the country's economic strategy, there would

*Traditional shipbuilding on Clydeside, 1945.*

The Trustees of the Imperial War Museum, London

Charles Mapleston

*Factory-based shipbuilding at Harland and Wolff in Belfast in 1987. This part of the new BP combined oil tanker and rig was constructed under cover and then lifted by crane into the dock to be welded to the other factory-made sections of the ship.*

inevitably have been a dramatic shift in the employment pattern away from engineering and towards the consumer goods industries. It would have been better to have recognised and accepted the trends at an earlier stage so that the shift away could have been better planned, and made less socially divisive and economically catastrophic. Corby, Consett and the Welsh Valleys are monuments to the speed of decline in places that have depended almost exclusively on one industry.

It is one thing to accept shrinkage in manufacturing industry, quite another to conclude that manufacturing industry is unimportant. Exactly the reverse is the case. Manufacturing remains an essential area of wealth creation. Those industries that are at the leading edge of technological change are particularly important for future prosperity.

It is a mistake to look to such industries to provide any substantial growth in direct employment. However, their indirect contribution to employment throughout the economy is fundamental and without it there would inevitably be a serious decline in living standards. Their role, in short, is the creation of wealth but not direct employment, and it is better to separate the two ideas. In the 21st century, employment in manufacturing may only account for 10 per cent of the total work force, but this will be enough to drive the economy as a whole.

This change in economic emphasis has widespread environmental repercussions. In urban areas the impact on land use is already visible. As employment has shrunk in relation to production so too has the use of space: more can be manufactured with fewer people and in less space. Modern industries also tend to cause less pollution. Gradually industrialists and planners are realising the potential of these changes. In each of the four cities, land is being released by industry for redevelopment on a huge scale. The land without exception is in a prime position for redevelopment. In Newcastle it borders the Tyne; in Southampton it looks out towards the leisure space of the Solent; in Belfast it sits between the city centre and the Lough; in Glasgow it follows the route of the Clyde. To the east of Glasgow and in places like Clydebank and Linwood the scale of the abandoned land could accommodate a whole country town. Elsewhere, in the West Midlands, Lancashire and the Swansea Valley, for example, are places where derelict industrial land must be the key to replanning and regeneration.

It is not only that these derelict areas are unsightly. They represent a wasting capital asset. Here is land that is no longer working for the community it serves. In design terms, potentially, such areas are the focus for new thinking and fresh initiatives. They are the essential space within cities in which to plan imaginatively for the future. This marks a significant change in policy. Since 1945 the planning frontier has been on ex-urban, greenfield sites and pre-eminently in the development of new towns. Now attention is switching to the rich mosaic of city life. Precisely when our cities need regeneration and renewal, the same industrial forces that led to their decline have provided space in which to redevelop. Former industrial sites can be used for new housing, the growing leisure and service sectors and clean new technologies.

Each of the four cities is using its derelict industrial land to change the geographical emphasis of the city. In Southampton and Belfast the effect will be to pull the centre towards the sea, by opening up a direct route on to the quayside and using it for shops, houses and leisure facilities. In Glasgow, the former tobacco warehousing area adjoining the hub of the city at George Square is being redeveloped for housing, restaurants and shops. This 'Merchant City' scheme is bringing people back to live in the urban heartland and dramatically raising the capital value of the redesigned and refurbished buildings. In Gateshead, the Garden Festival is being used as part of a strategy to regenerate and make accessible the banks of the River Tyne. The festival site is a heavily polluted area of derelict land and bringing it into use will depend on the imaginative employment of technology, engineering, planning, landscaping and architectural design. Turning these vast waste areas back into economic assets will provide large-scale employment in the construction industries.

Environmental and economic revival may, however, disadvantage some social groups. Sadly, these will often be the people with an original stake in the area, who may have lived and worked there all their lives. Former employees of the declined traditional industries may not want or be able to work in the new ones. As one old docker in Southampton put it: 'They're turning the place into a rich man's playground.' He said they couldn't all be barmen, Bingo callers or computer operators and that, in any case, a very large number of the new jobs were scandalously low-paid.

Few would agree that these areas should have been allowed to decline in the first place, but it is difficult to see how to re-create the traditional values of working-class solidarity which had its roots in local manufacturing work. The hope is that revived communities will emerge, consisting of a wide range of people. This is beginning to happen. The population of inner-city areas is now creeping up again but it is less evident that the newcomers are mixing with established residents who naturally regard the place as 'theirs'. New neighbours are not always welcome in old neighbourhoods.

What will these new areas look like? What will they be like to be in? One thing is clear: they will not resemble the massive re-development schemes of the 1960s and 1970s. That 'scorched earth' policy of flatten and build is now discredited. The conservationists have won the day so effectively that any buildings of architectural quality will, if at all possible, be retained and re-used. The commercial success of such pioneer schemes as St Katherine's Dock

***Abandoned dockside land, Southampton.***

Charles Mapleston

Charles Mapleston

*A group of dockers at Southampton said 'they're turning the place into a rich man's playground'. Much of the land abandoned by heavy industry will be used for leisure, tourism, housing and service industries. This will create employment – but of a new kind. The people who originally lived and worked in these places are not always the people to benefit from the new developments.*

in London has shown that history and architectural excellence are marketable commodities. This new respect for quality is also a triumph of ordinary common sense over professional arrogance. Local people have always regretted the loss of their famous landmarks; now their views are more respected. But, apart from the old buildings which are preserved, the new ones will be more diverse and varied than in the immediate past. Today's architects and planners are more catholic in their sources of influence, and the growth of what critics call 'post-Modernism' has made it respectable to design buildings that are playful and even eccentric. There is now an attempt to echo the character of the old in the new. Scale, materials and details will often follow the form of existing buildings or spaces.

The design principles behind the new approach have been set out in an excellent book called *Responsive Environments*. Its five authors[1] describe the qualities they are seeking by means of the following seven key ideas:

**Permeability** means providing a choice of routes, access points and views in a development. While balancing privacy against accessibility, this quality encourages people to explore, to linger and to meet unexpectedly.

**Variety** means mixing building forms, uses and meanings.

The authors explain what they want:

a place with varied uses has varied building

types of varied forms.

- it attracts varied people, at varied times, for varied reasons.
- because the different activities, forms and people provide a rich perceptual mix, different users interpret the place in different ways: it takes on varied meanings.

This conjures up the picture of a traditional market square where shops, offices, homes, public buildings, pubs, and the weekly market all co-exist harmoniously and create a place in which it is a pleasure to be.

**Legibility** means simply that it should be easy to find one's way around and places should explain their purpose by their form and appearance. This relates back to variety: particular buildings should have individuality and character which explains their function.

**Robustness** means that buildings and places should be adaptable. A city's buildings should be strong enough to accept change without too much upheaval. But the principle of robustness goes further. It is useful to provide adaptable spaces that can be used for different functions at different times of the day or year. Space in front of a pub or café will be valuable for customers in the summer but in winter it may be used by a hot-dog stall or a roast chestnuts vendor.

**Visual Appropriateness** Appearance 'is important because it strongly affects the interpretations people put on the place: whether designers want them to or not, people will interpret places as having meanings.' The suggestion is that the appearance of buildings should not simply reflect the architect's taste: rather it should use the symbols and details that everyone understands because they have been learnt in the process of growing up. It means paying attention to traditional forms.

**Richness** means 'designing for all the senses'. Although much discussion of design is conducted in visual terms, we also experience buildings and places through movement, smell, hearing and touch. Designers need to be aware of the potential richness of this sensory experience and to design for it. To demonstrate the point: in the re-creation of a Tudor garden in Southampton, the soft smell of the herbs and the warmth of the sun were as powerful as the visual delight of old walls, gravel paths and flowers.

**Personalisation** means designing buildings and places hoping that people will add to and change them, so making them their own.

These ideas are beginning to emerge, in some places more successfully than others. At their best the results are refreshing. Occasional lapses of taste and detail are easier to forgive than the brutality of mass concrete and the deadening uniformity of huge anonymous blocks. Architecture is struggling once again to provide the human scale, decoration and warm materials that people in our damp and cold islands have always wanted. Perhaps we might call this a revolutionary return to tradition.

Charles Mapleston

*Ocean Village, Southampton. This was once part of the thriving commercial port.*

(1) Ian Bentley, Alan Alcock, Paul Murrain, Sue McGlynn and Graham Smith. *Responsive Environments* was published by the Architectural Press, London, in 1985. ISBN 0 85139 967 3.

# BETTER LITTLE BOXES

There seems always to have been an element of snobbery in the attitude of people towards the idea of council houses. Yet from 1900 onwards, public housing of one kind or another led the field in terms of design. The garden cities, garden suburbs, the 'village green' style of layout and the varied architectural achievements of the first new towns, had their roots in a concern for the form and planning of homes for ordinary people, the majority of which were rented. At the end of the Second World War there was a determination to capitalise on this experience and create new council housing that would finally and decisively break with the slums of the past.

How could such a cherished dream have failed so utterly? Many of the places created to solve the housing problem are now slums themselves. Places like the Broadwater Farm Estate in Haringey, Hulme in Manchester and the notorious Divis Flats in Belfast have become synonymous with environmental disaster and social collapse. Increased powers for the police are being sought to combat the crime and rioting in exactly these areas of 'utopian' new building. The cure has finally proved horribly worse than the disease.

Newcastle and Glasgow both have huge problems arising directly from past council building policies. Belfast, uniquely, has put up a substantial number of new homes for rent since 1980 and has been able to learn valuable lessons from the mistakes made elsewhere. The new houses — designed, built and owned by the Northern Ireland Housing Executive — are probably the best to be found anywhere in the United Kingdom. Taken together, these three cities provide a fascinating insight into what went wrong and how it may be put right.

The degradation of much city council housing cannot be explained by any single cause. Management and design are both involved. Here, in no particular order, are some of the factors mentioned most frequently by tenants and officials alike:

- Unresponsive and remote management making it hard to get repairs done or social problems put right.
- Lack of maintenance of shared and public areas which quickly become a desert of trampled grass, broken glass and litter, and it is not clear whose responsibility it is to put them right.
- Huge areas of housing with no local amenities – no corner shops, pubs, clubs, sports halls, not even churches or rent offices! This means that residents do not meet each other socially and so a sense of community cannot easily develop. Often primary schools are the only truly local social amenities.
- Buildings that all look the same, that are brutal in scale or detailing and do not offer any scope for the people who live there to personalise them.
- Badly made buildings that, because of poor design and faulty construction, leak or encourage condensation and dampness. Many of these were put up in the 1960s and 1970s building boom and used untested methods of 'industrialised building'. They are proving an intractable problem even to keep watertight.
- Estates that, during the rush to build in the 1960s and 1970s, simply were not designed carefully enough; where buildings are poorly related to each other and to the site as a whole. Some are equally as bleak and dull as the apparently faceless streets they replaced.
- Tower blocks of truly frightening size and scale where inhuman design is linked to poor supervision and management so that lifts do not work for days at a time and old people and families can become virtual prisoners on the upper storeys.
- Deck-access flats where, because the decks do not 'belong' to anybody, they become filthy, vandalised and dangerous.
- Huge housing estates remote from city centres or work places entailing long and difficult daily journeys, big problems for old people and the isolation of teenagers in places with 'nothing to do'.
- The policy of concentrating so-called 'bad' tenants on single estates.
- The creation of vast areas of housing with only one form of tenancy and one social group.
- Residual problems from the days of massive slum clearance, when whole communities were broken up and moved with total disregard of their traditions, values and social ties.

Charles Mapleston

*Public housing dating from the immediate past is now the focus of much design work. Certain basic principles are emerging, including: providing private spaces; providing enclosed communal spaces; removing or replacing blocks, or lowering them; replacing leaky flat roofs by traditional pitched ones; breaking up access decks into private balconies. Jane Darbyshire's work on the Rochester Estate in Newcastle shows how this can be done. The picture shows how the estate looked shortly after abandonment. One block has already been demolished to provide space for gardens and car parks.*

The scale of the problem facing local authorities is daunting and is, in itself, only a part of the larger issue of housing in the United Kingdom. In 1985 the Association of Metropolitan Authorities' report, *Building for Tomorrow,* suggested that, for England alone, the following figures were involved:

| | | *Cost (£b)* |
|---|---|---|
| Crude housing shortage | 982 000 dwellings | 28.5 |
| Rehabilitation and repair of sub-standard housing | Private sector | 26.0 |
| | Public sector | 19.0 |
| | Total | 73.5 |

The Department of the Environment put the public sector bill for repair and rehabilitation at £18.8b, remarkably close to the AMA figure, but calculated in a completely different way.

In real terms government spending since 1979 on health and education and science has risen slightly, but on housing it has more than halved. Spending on social security and employment has grown substantially over the same period. However, the councils' own actions have sometimes contributed to their housing difficulties.

A complex of political influences is at work here and it is interesting to see how policies at local and national levels have interacted to exacerbate the problem. This is brought out very clearly in the Inquiry into Housing in Glasgow:

> 'In recent years government grant to public sector housing in Glasgow (housing support grant) has been sharply reduced from £73m in 1980/81 to £25m in 1986/87 (at 1985/86 prices). Rate fund contributions to housing have been reduced by some £20m over a five year period. . . . This process, coupled with a resistance to rent increases, has seriously eroded the financial base for housing repair and maintenance services in the public sector.

*Architects' drawing of the scheme.*

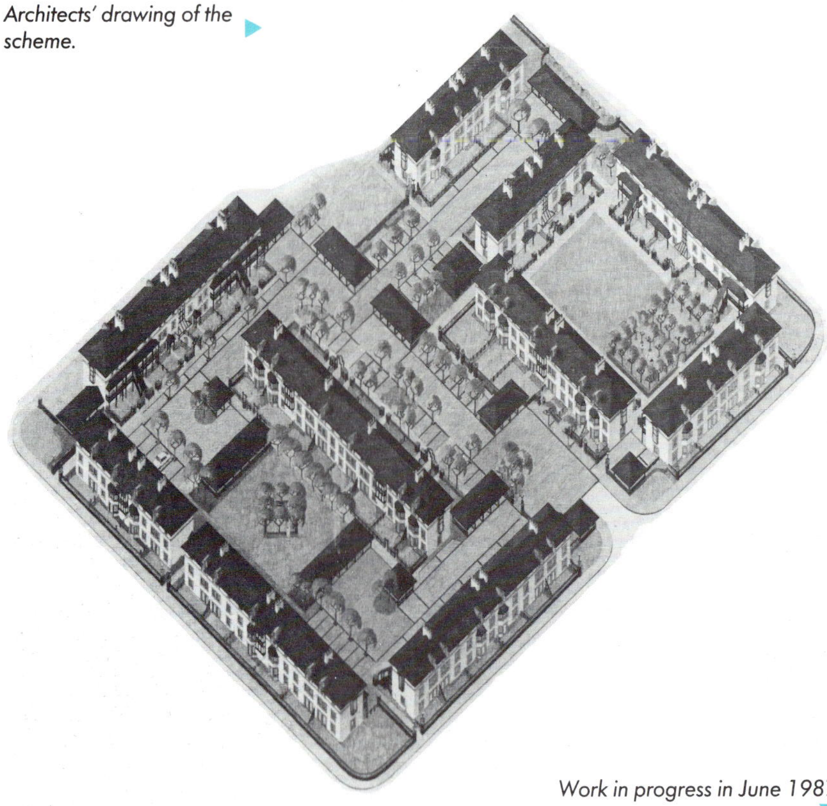

*Work in progress in June 1987.*

Charles Mapleston

Inadequate, routine repair and maintenance practices in the public sector have . . . contributed to stock deterioration. . . . Whilst this is in part due to restrictions on capital allocations, the effect of the council's low rent policy should not be understated. If Glasgow rents had been the same as average rents in England and Wales between 1971 and 1985 an additional £211m would have been available for repair and maintenance work, 6 times the current annual repairs budget for Glasgow.'

This begs the question of the council's responsibility for the poorest members of its community, but it also shows dramatically that money for house building and repair can only be generated by an effective economy – whether the resulting wealth is recycled into the environment through public or private spending. In an area of economic decline and high unemployment, rents are likely to be low and environmental standards consequently fall.

Paul Mugnaioni, Glasgow's Director of Housing, believes that at present levels of spending it will be impossible for the council to keep its existing stock in even minimal repair, let alone carry out an acceptable programme of redesign and reconstruction. The Inquiry says that this is a problem of national importance for Scotland and that the eventual price for ignoring it, in terms of money and disruption, will get higher each year. Anyone visiting the actual places represented by the statistics would find it a dismaying experience. The environmental quality of these disadvantaged areas is a disgrace by any standard.

If the necessary resources become available, do we now have the knowledge and skill to use them intelligently? Can we avoid the mistakes of the past? The evidence is that we can. There is a new understanding of the crucial relationship between designing and managing public housing. Put at its very simplest, it means finding out what people want and giving it to them, because they will look after it and value it. What most families want is a modest house with their own front door and a small garden. This now seems to apply even in Glasgow where the tradition has been to live in a flat or tenement. Some single people and young and older couples may prefer flats, but in blocks of more

Charles Mapleston

*Barrowfield Estate. In this scheme to landscape the back courts of a decayed 1930s estate the tenants have been given full control. They commissioned the designer and got what they wanted. As this is an area of high unemployment a condition of getting the contract is to employ local labour. The design work is only a part of a tremendous effort by local people to improve their area and renew their community.*

modest, human scale and of welcoming appearance, with well-maintained grounds and perhaps a resident manager or caretaker. Exactly what private owners expect and frequently get!

It is one thing to recognise these ideals but quite another to transform the exising stock of poor council housing to meet requirements. Much of the worst building consists of leaky, systems-built deck-access flats and tower blocks. These may look unpromising, but in both Newcastle and Glasgow there is a clear idea of what needs to be done and the initial results are encouraging. Similar approaches are proving effective in London, and planners from as far afield as Hong Kong and New York are learning from Glagow's example.

In tackling the worst design aspects of the stock of council flats the most typical approaches combine two or more of the following elements:

— Demolition of selected blocks to create a less oppressive setting on a reduced scale.
— Lowering the height of selected blocks so that they become suitable for conversion into separate houses, or allow a better mix of houses and flats.
— Improving inadequate structural work and providing effective heat conservation.
— Replacing flat, leak-prone roofs, with

traditional sloping ones: this is obviously functional in the British climate and it dramatically changes the block's appearance, making even quite large buildings look more like the accepted image of a house.

- Dividing up the decks of deck-access flats so that each flat has a separate, private entrance. In the best examples, the deck then becomes a private balcony.
- Creating private gardens and semi-private fenced or walled spaces where children can play in safety.
- Improving planting, fencing and paving: making the place less 'municipal'.
- Where the original buildings were standardised, making deliberate use of varied finishes and details so that there is more sense of individuality.
- Converting some houses or flats into community facilities or corner shops.
- Changing internal layouts to provide modern space standards for people and the large range of consumer goods some of them will own.
- Encouraging personalisation and participation so that the process of design is continual, as tenants take over from where the professionals leave off.

In terms of management, Glasgow has made a successful start in decentralising its repair and letting services, and at Red Road Tower the council has transformed a tower block simply by refurbishing it thoroughly, changing the letting pattern and installing a brilliantly competent manageress with a small support staff. These management changes are part of a national realisation that it pays to bring tenants back into

Charles Mapleston

*Red Road Tower. Here the homes of tenants have been transformed by refurbishment, new security systems and the installation of an excellent manageress on site. So far only one tower has been treated in this way.*

Charles Mapleston

*Refurbished Barratt homes for sale on one of Glasgow's peripheral estates at Easterhouse.*

the management of their own communities, and indeed into the design process.

In 1986 this new movement found corporate expression at a conference entitled 'Building Communities'. Attention was drawn to the following section of the 1981 Scarman Report on the Brixton riots:

> 'Local communities should be more fully involved in the decisions which affect them. A 'top-down' approach to regeneration does not seem to have worked. Local communities must be fully and effectively involved in planning, in the provision of local services, and in the managing and financing of specific projects. . . . Inner city areas are not human deserts. They possess a wealth of voluntary effort and good will. It would be wise to put this human capital to good use. . . . It is essential that people are encouraged to secure a stake in, feel a pride in, and have a sense of responsibility for their own area.'

One of the best ways of achieving this involvement is to give people the power to change their own environment. They decide how it will develop and because that decision is based on intimate local knowledge, it is likely to be effective. The environment works better if the people who live, work and play in it are involved in its creation and management. This is not the same as saying that tenants should become amateur planners or architects, but that they should become the *real* clients. The tenants should have the power to develop the brief with architects, planners and engineers and to engage in a debate with them in exactly the same way that a private client would. They should have a final say in the decisions that will affect them and their community.

Some planners and politicians fear that ordinary people will not have the wisdom and far-sightedness to take sensible design decisions. But there is much evidence to the contrary. The residents of Barrowfield and Calvay in Glasgow, and Loadman Street in Newcastle, for instance, worked very successfully with their architects. They influenced what was done, and by co-ordinating design, management and community dévelopment created a climate of involvement and excitement which could not have been achieved in any other way.

In Northern Ireland there has been a huge programme of new house building over the past seven years. Very little council housing was put up in Ulster between the wars, and even after 1945 progress was relatively slow, despite a considerable back-log. But there was an additional impetus to the building programme. One of the driving forces behind the sectarian troubles which erupted violently again in 1969 was a feeling of grievance about housing conditions. It therefore became a matter of public policy to eradicate housing shortages and bad conditions. In 1971 a new body — the Northern Ireland Housing Executive — was set up to remove housing provision from the responsibility of the possibly sectarian local authorities. At the outset, its brief was hardly to revolutionise the quantity and quality of public housing in the Province. It took some time to convince Whitehall that housing conditions in Northern Ireland lagged dangerously and scandalously behind those on the mainland. At present Ulster, and particularly Belfast, is the United Kingdom's living laboratory for new approaches to housing design. Well built, pleasantly proportioned, nicely detailed brick houses, mainly with small gardens, are grouped around friendly, human-scale, urban courtyards or squares from which through-traffic is excluded. In Ulster, as people of different religious persuasions prefer not to live together, the concept of 'defensible space' has a sharp and real significance. The grouping of the new

*The state of the existing buildings at Easterhouse with one of the refurbished Barratt houses in the background.*

Charles Mapleston

buildings reinforces this: each community being locked safely within its boundaries.

The flourishing design developments in Ulster are not matched by community participation of the kind now emerging in England, Scotland and Wales. But it is fascinating to note that what benevolent paternalism has achieved in Belfast's new public housing matches so closely the aspirations of grass-roots tenants groups on the mainland. In both cases what is wanted is a real house: a house that looks and feels like the traditional picture of a house, with all modern amenities, space to park a car, and at least a patch of garden; a house with space outside where children can play in safety, and an enclosed town square or village green. In the past, the United Kingdom has always struck visitors by its unique adherence to individual small houses, whereas on the Continent, for instance, people seem happy living in large blocks of flats. Evidently, we are beginning to make a successful return to our indigenous design roots: an environment of varied, nicely detailed, very domestic buildings of modest size. It is one in which most of us feel at home.

*The Lough Lea Estate in Belfast. Northern Ireland has some of the best new public housing in the United Kingdom. It is based on good traditional designs and materials. Over the past decade Ulster, and in particular Belfast, has been something of a laboratory for the way housing design may go in the future.*

# ADDING VALUE

Industry makes its profits and stays in business by 'adding value' to raw materials or components which, before being processed, may be quite cheap. Designing is at the centre of this process because it is the activity that decides what form the resulting products will take. The products that embody this 'added value' must be ones that people actually want at a price they are willing to pay. The buyer, whether an individual or a corporation, has to share the same perception of value as the manufacturer if a deal is to be made. This principle can be extended to all transactions, whether relating to services, leisure or the environment.

Providing something people want at the price they are willing to pay is actually quite difficult, and, up until recently, the United Kingdom has not been particularly good at it. This is partly due to the nature of existing plant, and partly a matter of attitudes. The consequences of many years of undercapitalisation will be experienced in the 1990s, for it is quite clear that only modern, highly productive plant can compete in terms of cost and quality. There have been many decades of parochialism: years of saying 'we've always made it like that'; of seeing the home market as a microcosm of the world market; and of not recognising trends in world markets far enough in advance. And we have not been good enough at identifying and creating new markets for ourselves.

Since the 1960s, UK manufacturing companies have attempted time and again to remain in familiar but declining markets where there has inevitably been over-provision and, as a result, savage competition. There has been a matching failure to compete on anything but cost. Unfortunately, we cannot compete on cost in shrinking markets because countries in the developing world have unchallengeable price advantages in terms of labour and plant. But there is an added problem. Many technological products and consumer goods are now purchased on quality rather than cost and our manufacturers have been slow to realise this fact and to capitalise on it. In the 1950s and 1960s when our industries should have been moving into the production of high quality, high technology goods with a big margin of sales price over costs, they were, in fact, fighting a series of rearguard actions based on lowering the price and quality of essentially old-fashioned products.

Managements have tended to despise and stratify their workforces while unions have frequently been inflexible. These tendencies have priced us out of one market after another. What is important for the future is to recognise those areas in which we can compete and to do this on a world-wide rather than on a local basis. The following case studies are examples where a market has been recognised and captured and in which design has played a crucial role.

**James Howden, Glasgow**
A traditional engineering company that has analysed world markets for what they call 'new new' products. From 320 possible market opportunities, five have been selected for development and all show promise of success. Sophisticated design and outstandingly modern (and continuously modernised) plant are linked to an effective system of computer-aided design and manufacture. There have been no redundancies for 10 years. Their wind generator, for example, appears to have solved the problem of economic large-scale wind power for electricity generation and is already the market leader in the United States, where Howden's had an assembly plant and now sell electricity to the local generating board. They have just won the contract to supply boring machines for the 'Chunnel'.

**Fast Engineering, Muckamore, near Belfast**
A small, exemplary business established by Seamus Connolly and employing 10 people. Connolly's experience in civil engineering led him to recognise the need for cheap, light, transportable water tanks. His design is entirely original. It uses a collapsible lightweight aluminium frame to support a heavy plastic container. Each tank can be erected in 5 minutes. The original tanks, and new related designs, are used all over the world by relief agencies, oil companies, fire services and fish farmers. Connolly's company is using the same technology to produce a trampoline for the domestic market.

**Stoddard Carpets, Johnstone, Renfrewshire**
A large and well-established company which has used design and technology to capture a large slice of the market for contract carpeting.

Charles Mapleston

Charles Mapleston

*Erecting one of the portable watertanks made by Fast Engineering near Belfast. This well-designed product is exported all over the world by the company which is itself a model of what a well-organised small business should be. Businesses of this kind have a central role to play in the future economy of Britain's cities.*

Understanding changes in interior design, introducing novel machinery, developing new printing techniques and accurately forecasting changes in taste in interior design are among the ingredients of its success. Profitability for Stoddard depends on producing a better designed and made product, capable of commanding a substantial premium over production costs. In its old ranges the company was making and selling large amounts of carpet but only generating a very small profit. Design has helped to increase the premium of value over cost by two and a half times.

**Spence Bryson, Belfast**
Linen and shipbuilding were fundamental to the growth of Belfast. Both have since declined but are now struggling to re-establish themselves as industries with a future. For linen this has meant recognising that entering the international fashion market depends on excellent design and that fresh designs are needed every year. Spence Bryson, an old established firm, is expanding in the fashion field with the help of its new design consultant, Beryl Gibson.

The environment is looked at in the same way: places where design has played its part in 'adding value' to buildings or land and so has brought them back into effective and economically viable use.

**Shamrock Quay, Southampton**
This was a traditional yacht building yard working to very high craft standards and steadily losing money. The yard was bought by Dean and Dyball, a company involved in engineering and property development. They have converted it into a boating centre where yacht owners can bring their craft to obtain the services of the group of small specialist companies based there. Restaurants, shops and offices form part of the complex which hums with life and enterprise. This is a development that has rejuvenated a group of fine buildings that were about to be abandoned, and created work in manufacturing, service and leisure industries.

**Loadman Street, Newcastle**
Ralph Erskine's famous Byker Estate has provided the inspiration for a variety of public housing developments in Newcastle, many of which involve co-operation between the public, private and co-operative sectors. These developments are fundamentally design-led. Structural changes, humanising and personalising the appearance of buildings and providing private space are all ideas with their roots in the Byker scheme. At Loadman Street the district council is working with the local tenants and Newcastle Architecture Workshop to refurbish a group of grim deck-access flats which resulted from the 1970s building boom. Here tenants are involved before the design work begins and have a say in its progress. The

Northern Ireland Tourist Office

*The Opera House, Belfast. Refurbishing this splendid old building helped to restore life into the centre of the city.*

Architecture Workshop maintains and interprets the dialogue between the designers and the tenants. Had the estate not been recovered in this way, it would have entered a period of final decay and may have been demolished.

**Belfast City Centre**

The shopping and entertainment area of Belfast's centre is one of the few places where the divided community meets. Up until the mid-1970s, however, it was normally empty after the working day. The drifting away of shoppers and, even more so, people seeking leisure and entertainment had brought economic decline and further environmental decay. The Northern Ireland Department of the Environment then initiated a deliberate campaign to bring the area back to life. Urban and architectural design were the focus of the enterprise that involved, among other things, pedestrianisation of certain streets, conservation of a fine old building owned by Marks & Spencer and the skilful refurbishment of the Opera House by the Arts Council. The campaign has been remarkably effective: people and commerce have returned and the environment has been transformed.

## Changes in Technology

These promising developments in manufacturing and the environment show a sharp awareness of the technological, economic and social changes that are influencing the world economy in general and the United Kingdom in particular. There seems to be general agreement about the nature of the changes. Many of the planners, manufacturers and designers interviewed for the programmes spoke of the same group of influences. Here are some of the elements that were mentioned most regularly:

- The speed of technological developments and their influence in making products, plant and skills obsolete but also the opportunities for new technologically based products.
- The growth of leisure and service industries and the opportunities for manufacturers to create new products to serve those industries.
- The new potential of the leisure and service industries to be the cutting edge of environmental improvement.
- The importance of quality and design as major influences on buyers of heavy engineering, high technology, consumer and fashion goods, and housing.
- The continued expansion of retailing to serve the growing disposable income of those people in work. It is this expansion that is making possible much of the current wave of city centre building and regeneration.

*The Metro Centre, Gateshead. The success of closed shopping areas has been one of the most striking developments in town design in the 1980s.*

Charles Mapleston

Charles Mapleston

*The Burrell Art Gallery, Glasgow. The establishment of this magnificent collection in its own gallery was one of a number of new developments that have changed the image of the city and made it a centre for tourism. It is to be cultural capital of Europe in 1990 — a tribute to new-found confidence and excellent environmental design.*

- A recognition of the importance of 'knowledge' or 'information' as the basis for future products and services. Many people emphasised the significance of creating new links between education, training, research and industry.

Working against these forces for expansion and economic success are a number of equally well-defined difficulties:

- A growing divide between rich and poor, resulting in declining services and bad environmental quality in concentrated pockets of disadvantage.
- The social injustice and unrest caused by the strains of prolonged unemployment due to the change from a traditional manufacturing economy to high technology and service industries.
- Underlying world-wide problems of poverty, the depletion of non-renewable resources, and pollution. The rich, industrialised nations will have to recognise these pressures and share responsibility for them.
- The psychological and educational problems of moving from a traditional manufacturing economy to one in which wealth is created

through knowledge, technology, design skills, leisure and services. The UK education system is struggling to catch up.
— The legacy of a declining, old-fashioned and frequently badly maintained infrastructure of roads, railways, water supply, schools, hospitals and houses.

It is, of course, not only up to designers to contribute towards improving the situation. The problem is also political and economic, social and psychological. Having said this, the scope for a positive design contribution is considerable.

Some opportunities are being effectively exploited by design in the struggle to regenerate industry, employment and the urban environment. These opportunities arise from change, and grasping them means accepting change. Fundamentally, these changes come from developments in technology that are affecting the nature and distribution of work. The process has destroyed traditional markets but it has created new ones. Penetrating these new markets depends on design in the most fundamental sense of the word. It requires us to imagine how the future will be and to provide the products, places and services that people will need.

It is evident that there are excellent designers and managers in the field who understand the fundamental character of the industrial and environmental changes now facing us. However, it is doubtful if they have the resources necessary to make use of all the opportunities that exist. As we saw, Glasgow will need £140m per year for the next 10 years, simply to keep the public housing stock in repair. To bring it up to an acceptable environmental design standard will cost a further £100m per year for 10 years. If this figure is not met, the buildings will have to be pulled down or they will sink into social and structural chaos. At present the district council has £64m per year to spend, though it is supplementing this by imaginative schemes for co-operating with the private sector. As new government policies emerge, it seems certain that further resources will become available.

The shift to leisure and service industries is dramatic and it is not clear that enough has been done to assist that process through re-training and help with personal mobility. What is more, these industries depend heavily on design. The 'image' of a place, its attractiveness and effectiveness, are 'values added' – not only by the graphic design of advertising but by the creation of new and dramatic structures. These structures will determine whether a place visited once will be visited again. And there are jobs to be created by making and maintaining the products that support leisure, entertainment and education.

At the same time, the nature of manufacturing industry has been transformed. It no longer needs thousands upon thousands of metal bashers, housed in dark satanic mills, watched over by a hostile management and guarded by Luddite unions. Tomorrow's metal bashers may well need a degree to operate their computer-controlled machinery. But more than that, this new industry will have to be oriented towards the market, to understand what people need and will buy; towards technology, to recognise what can be made at a price people can afford; and towards design, to create the form of products that will link together what people need with what technology can achieve.

# A CHANGING ECONOMY

CHANGES IN NUMBERS EMPLOYED 1971 1985

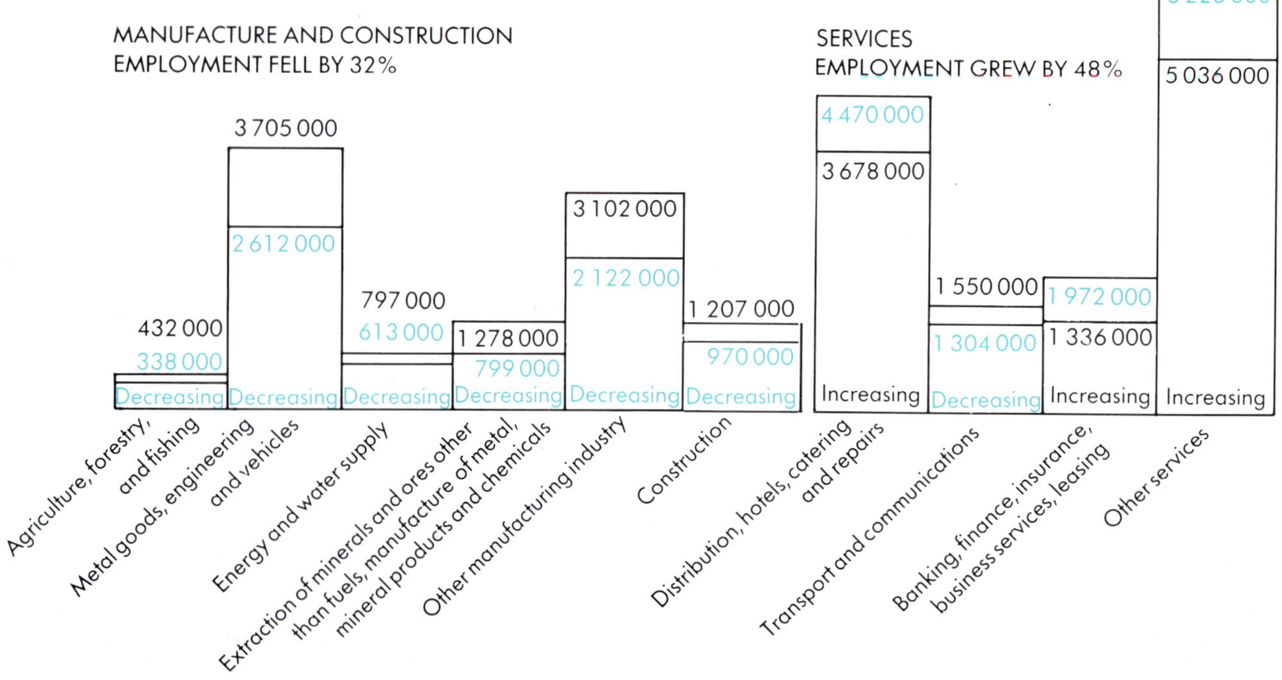


REDUNDANCY RATES PER 1000 BY AREA OF EMPLOYMENT

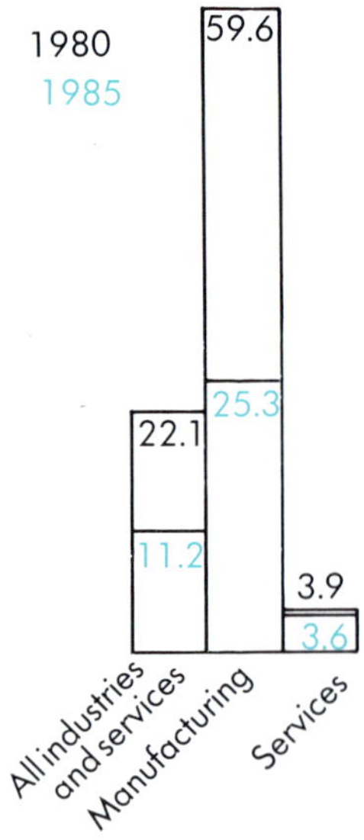


CHANGES IN CONSUMER SPENDING (£ million) 1980 = 100

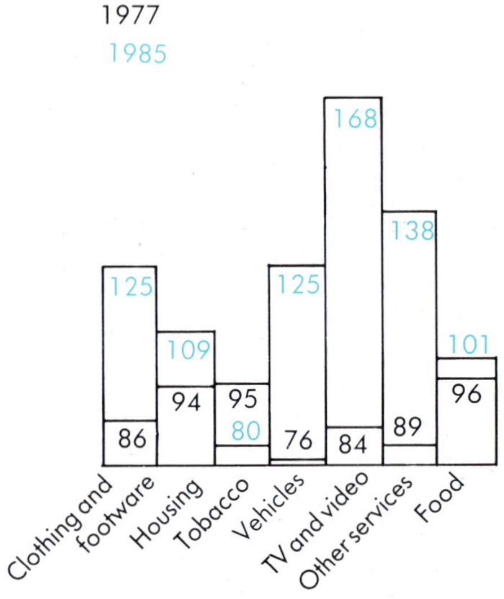


CHANGES IN UK HOUSE OWNERSHIP ( million)

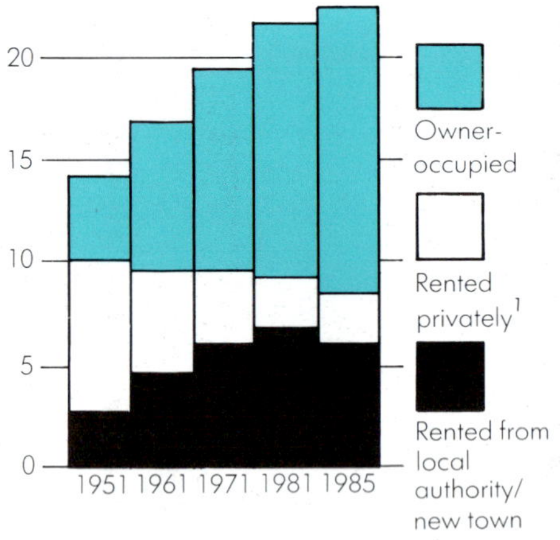


*Note: All figures from* Social Trends 17, *HMSO 1987.*

[1] Includes housing associations and dwellings rented with farm or business premises, and those occupied by virtue of employment.

# BELFAST FACTS AND FIGURES

Population of the Belfast City Council area is 343 000. However, the city is the immediate centre for about 500 000 people living around Belfast Lough and along the valley formed by the River Lagan. A little under half of the population of Northern Ireland lives within easy commuting distance of the city centre.

The population of the city area has declined steadily since 1971 when it was 415 000. This decline is now halting.

The rate of unemployment is very high: 21 per cent.

The city centre has attracted huge investment since the low point of the mid-1970s. In 1984 it was estimated that around £60m of new investment was planned for the shopping area, including Marks & Spencer's hugely successful £18m extension.

Only 50 per cent of all households in the urban area own a car.

In 1979 a House Condition Survey concluded that 25 per cent of the stock in Belfast was in need of major improvement: 15 per cent was unfit. Since then £1.25b has been spent and the statistics have been transformed to half their previous levels.

Belfast shares with the rest of Northern Ireland fundamental social and economic differences to England, Scotland and Wales:

Forty-eight per cent of all workers are employed directly by the state.

Public spending is between 30 and 40 per cent higher than the UK average.

Incomes are about 30 per cent below the UK average.

Charles Mapleston

*Belfast at night. The city is in a splendid natural site, surrounded by hills and with the River Lagan running through the centre of the built-up area.*

Harland & Wolff

Workers leave Harland and Wolff's great yard.

'Kitchen houses' in Raphael Street, 1912.

Ulster Museum

Belfast at the height of its prosperity was a city of contrasts. The wealth that came from ships and linen provided good employment, but it was not evenly distributed. In particular, Belfast's housing gradually fell behind the standards provided elsewhere in the United Kingdom.

Belfast has one of the most attractive settings of any city in the United Kingdom. It stands at the end of the Lough in a dish of splendid hills. But it is not a conventionally beautiful city. Although it received its Royal Charter from James I in 1613, the Industrial Revolution was responsible for its shape and character. Two great industries — linen and shipbuilding — were the engines that drove the expansion of the city and formed its environment. Between 1850 and 1900 the population rose dramatically — from 100 000 to 350 000. By the early 1950s it had reached 450 000. The city had a number of fine public buildings but visually was dominated by the huge linen mills, sailing like great ships through the sea of tiny red-brick 'kitchen houses' which housed the workforce. By the Lough, real ships dominated the scene in Harland and Wolff's prosperous shipyard.

Sectarian violence has destroyed people and property here for many years so that the city is criss-crossed by both visible and invisible boundaries of history and sentiment. This intangible geography is of course more vivid to those who have helped to create it, but even for the visitor it is a reality to be reckoned with. And it does affect design. Land in Ulster becomes something much more intractable. It becomes territory. What might provoke controversy in most European cities can result in violence here. Efforts to relieve the pressure of overcrowding in Catholic West Belfast, for example, are

*High Street in 1906 showing the new trams introduced in December 1905.*

Ulster Museum

*Suburban housing on the new estate at Poleglass, south of the city.*

Northern Ireland Housing Executive

hampered because no Protestant land may be used to solve the problem.

In the 1960s it seemed as though the growth of Belfast might continue unchecked. In 1964 it was believed that the population would be 760 000 in 1986. As we now know, economic forces have gone against this and, in fact, the 1960s proved to have been the end of a period of growth rather than the start of one. For Belfast this period of economic standstill coincided with a new outbreak of 'the Troubles'. One strand in this was resentment over discrimination in the allocation of local authority housing but the causes and motivations of the explosion were complex and perhaps even now are not well understood. By the early 1970s there was no good news to be heard in Belfast as industry, tourism and the quality of the environment declined, commensurate with the rising tide of violence and destruction. Only a decade after planners had been predicting its continued growth and prosperity the city was faced with:

- high unemployment
- the decline of traditional manufacturing industries
- the decay and destruction of urban housing, particularly developments built to meet the population explosion of the 19th century
- an ageing population as the young and able moved out
- increased dereliction
- changing shopping patterns away from the dangerous city centre to the suburbs
- Belfast's share of world economic recession.

Because this situation fed on the sectarian violence and in turn fed it, improving the Belfast environment became a matter of political importance. By-passing the local authorities, the

*It has been government policy to bring life back into the city centre. Old buildings have been carefully restored and refurbished. New buildings are designed to match the old in scale and detailing. Here the round-topped windows of the new Post Office echo those of the neighbouring building.*

Northern Ireland Department of the Environment and the Housing Executive embarked on a plan that must have seemed utopian in the mid-1970s but which, in fact, has proved remarkably effective.

Here, roughly in order of priority, is what the Government set out to do:

1 Improve housing conditions. The situation in Belfast was one of the worst in the United Kingdom. The Housing Executive embarked on a massive programme of new building in the city, supplemented by new suburbs. One, at Poleglass, shows very clearly the approach to design that the Executive has made its own: well-proportioned, individual houses with gardens are grouped around pleasant public spaces.

2 Bring life back into the centre of the city. This process began in two ways: encouraging multinational chains to invest in new shops, and encouraging the refurbishment of individual buildings. Everyone speaks of the renewal of the Opera House by the Arts Council of Northern Ireland as a turning point for the city. Certain areas within the 'Security Zone' have now been sensitively pedestrianised and the new buildings are of good architectural quality. On evenings when there is late-night shopping the city hums with life: 10 years ago it was deserted by 5.30pm.

3 Use wasting resources to create new employment. Here the creation of the Belfast Enterprise Zones are intended to do the job. In a number of cases they are based around once-empty linen mills, in others they are housed in new buildings constructed in the waste areas that divide one community from another. Small business is growing and the

Charles Mapleston

Ulster Museum

*Filming the Lagan area, which is presently derelict, and used by a scrap metal merchant on the banks of the Lagan, only a stone's throw from the city centre.*

*The river as it was in 1895.*

traditional industries of linen and engineering seem to have reached a degree of stability, though their ability to survive will depend on meeting very powerful international competition.

4 Make better use of the Lough and the River Lagan. This is a development for the future and it will change the relationship between the city and the sea by reclaiming from industry large waterside areas close to the city centre. The plan calls for massive investment, and attracting it will depend on investors being impressed by the success of what has already been done.

The tranformation of housing and the city centre are great achievements. They show the energy, skill and determination of civil servants and professionals who are struggling to improve the environment in the teeth of destructive forces. In subtle ways, planning and design find themselves reflecting the realities of the sectarian problem. More and more the shape of the environment adapts itself to the division between the two communities. Perhaps, for the moment at least, it is the only contribution that good design can offer towards making the people of the Province feel secure.

# GLASGOW FACTS AND FIGURES

In the 1981 census the population of the Strathclyde Region was 2 398 500. Glasgow is clearly the centre of this region and the Clyde bisects it. However it includes several predominantly rural areas. The population of the urban or industrial districts between the City of Glasgow and the mouth of the river were as follows:

| | |
|---|---|
| City of Glasgow | 767 500 |
| Clydebank | 52 400 |
| Dumbarton | 78 100 |
| Inverclyde | 100 900 |
| Renfrew | 209 200 |

The population of the city has declined since 1961 when the census figure was 1 140 000.

It is not hard to find statistics that point to the scale of Clydeside's problems, both relatively and absolutely. The graphs that follow, however, highlight the situation dramatically. Taken from the 1981 Census report, they show that the city area had more population loss and more unemployment per head of population than any other category of district in the Census.

*Port Glasgow, near the mouth of the Clyde, in 1768. An artist sits drawing on the hillside overlooking the harbour full of trading ships.*

The Mitchell Library

PERCENTAGE CHANGE IN POPULATION 1971–81 BY CATEGORY OF DISTRICT (AVERAGE FOR GREAT BRITAIN = 0.6%)

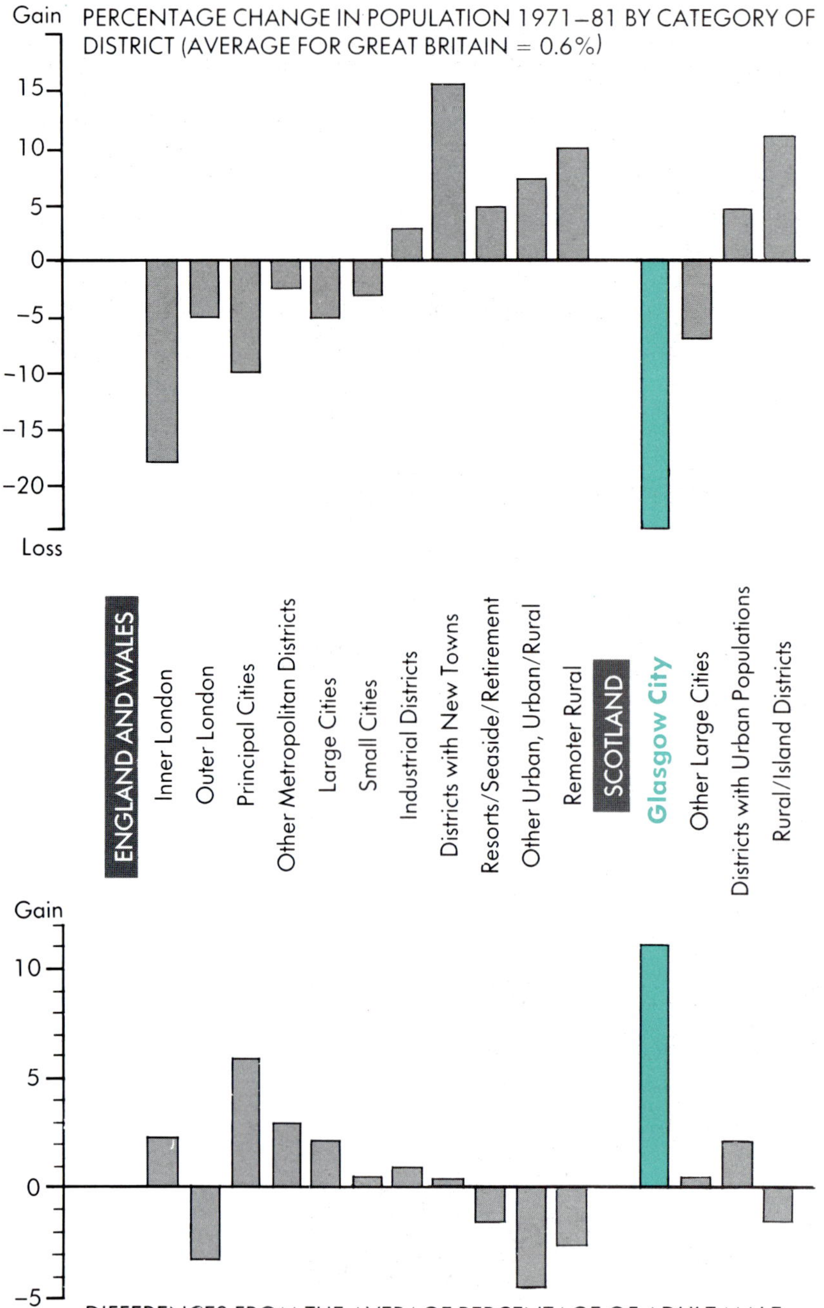


DIFFERENCES FROM THE AVERAGE PERCENTAGE OF ADULT MALE UNEMPLOYMENT IN 1981 BY CATEGORY OF DISTRICT (AVERAGE FOR GREAT BRITAIN = 10.5%)

Clydeside is no stranger to changing fortunes. Its economic heart is the city of Glasgow, where the first wave of prosperity was based on trade in textiles and tobacco. When it ebbed, Glasgow's engineers led the Industrial Revolution: by 1860 Britain was known as 'The Workshop of the World', and the Clyde was central to this reputation, making ships, locomotives and machinery for the Empire, Russia and South America. 'Clyde-built' meant not only well-crafted products but technical leadership as well. These 19th-century engineering designers could feel the pulse of world economic change and they built exactly what the market needed.

In 100 years all this had gone. Wave after wave of competition toppled Clydeside's supremacy. Glasgow was competing in markets where competition was desperately fierce. The great steel-using traditional industries declined. Companies that had been household names vanished. The loss of jobs and markets seemed irrevocable and even new initiatives, like the Rootes car plant at Linwood, quickly failed. By the early 1970s Glasgow's image was that of Europe's supreme problem city. Every statistic, social as well as economic, bore this out. Here was a picture of old-fashioned industries, poor housing, bad general health standards, an ugly, scarred environment: Glasgow was no place in which to be.

In a decade the picture has changed. Glasgow has revitalised its image and shed a glow over the whole surrounding region. There is a new industrial confidence among young Scots designers and engineers; environmental decline has been reversed and the area is grabbing a healthy and steadily expanding slice of the tourist market. The District Council has begun work on what is one of the largest and most intractable housing problems in the industrial world. People are moving back to live in the once decaying city centre.

The role of designers in these developments has been central. Designers have helped to create a new image for Glasgow in the 'Miles Better' campaign and given that image substance in new and refurbished buildings, a revitalised townscape and new products and services. In the immediate future two imaginative design projects stand out as symbols of

*The Clyde became the workshop of the world as the Industrial Revolution gained strength. Although recessions began to affect the engineering industries after the First World War, 'Clyde-built' continued to have a proud ring into the 1950s and 1960s. However, this masked old-fashioned design and archaic working practices. These industries were operating in a savagely competitive market and they did not survive.*

Glasgow's changing economy: the Garden Festival on old shipbuilding land on the South Bank of the Clyde, and the re-opening of part of the Forth and Clyde Canal as a tourist attraction.

But Glasgow is not Southampton and there is a tough realisation in the city that it is necessary to remain in the business of designing and making successful products. The plan here is not to go over to a service economy but to add an effective, lively, energetic leisure and tourist element to a city that already boasts fine museums and art galleries. The plan seems to be working. Without relinquishing its traditional aggressiveness and humour, Glasgow is now a place that is good to visit. It has the dignity, scale and roughness of a genuinely great city.

Redevelopment of the city centre conceals the true dimensions of Glasgow's housing problem. It is not only the inner-city areas which make up the GEAR project that need attention. The problems of the huge peripheral estates, created during the slum clearances of the 1950s and 1960s, are even more horrendous. The District Council has been able to identify the policies that could lead to an improvement but

'Doge's Palace', an old carpet factory on Glasgow Green, has become a splendid block of offices.

Charles Mapleston

Glasgow's derelict city centre sites are now being filled. Building goes ahead where St Enoch Station once stood.

Charles Mapleston

Charles Mapleston

*Excellent council housing from the 1930s.*

has not the necessary resources to carry them out on a sufficiently large scale. Unless more resources can be made available, these areas, already in headlong decline, will become impossible to save. Glasgow's housing problem constitutes an environmental and social crisis of massive proportions.

The Inquiry into Housing in Glasgow noted that 'the peripheral estates are in many ways the key housing problem in Glasgow' and it made a clear link between environmental improvement and economic development. It is worth quoting its recommendations in full:

1 The Council should be prepared to transfer, for full modernisation, up to 20 000 Council houses, 50 per cent of the peripheral estate stock, to locally based housing associations, housing co-operatives and to home ownership. Stock transfer on this large scale is necessary to create the fundamental change in housing conditions and management which are required in the peripheral areas. Responsive and intensive neighbourhood based housing management should be introduced into areas which remain predominantly in Council ownership. Improvement to these houses should be funded through the Council's capital programme. Full community involvement in the development of improvement and management proposals for each scheme is essential to ensure a high level of tenant commitment to the future of the areas concerned.

Charles Mapleston

Charles Mapleston

▲

▲

*Calvay Crescent in Barlanack as it was in 1986. The Calvay area is being redeveloped by a 'par-value co-operative' in which the tenants have nominal ownership of the estate and commission their own architect, solicitor and quantity surveyor.*

▲

*The result is a copy-book example of community architecture in action.*

3 Management improvements and successful modernisation by co-operatives and housing associations will provide a basis for the encouragement of home ownership through Council house sales and bring additional resources to assist the renewal of the estates. Private developers have already illustrated the potential for low cost owner occupation in such areas and should be encouraged to improve further housing for sale. The local authority should, however, ensure that adequate financial advice is freely available to house buyers and that the full financial obligations of house purchase are understood.

4 Environmental improvement is essential to help change the image of the peripheral estates, to reduce trespass, improve security and to improve amenities for residents. Environmental work must be regarded as an integral part of the housing improvement programme. It will require as much, if not greater, detailed design and management consideration by the community as dwelling space improvements themselves.

5 Economic, industrial and social programmes are beyond the remit of this Inquiry and clearly are vital to the successful renewal of the estates. Our resource proposals envisage additional expenditure of some £85m on non-housing projects including economic development projects. These resources should be channelled mainly through the SDA who are specialists in the field of industrial development and who should seek to involve private sector and venture capital resources fully. A clear link between development of the local economy and large scale housing expenditure should be made to ensure maximum benefit to the local community through direct employment and other means.

The ultimate health of Glasgow, and the key to its future, lies in its ability to transform the dismal, dangerous, boring and ugly places where so many of its inhabitants currently live.

# NEWCASTLE UPON TYNE FACTS AND FIGURES

The population of Tyneside in the 1981 census was as follows:

| | |
|---|---|
| Gateshead | 213 200 |
| Newcastle upon Tyne | 283 900 |
| North Tyneside | 198 500 |
| South Tyneside | 161 900 |

The population of all these districts has declined since 1961: at that time the population of Newcastle upon Tyne was 336 400.

Tyneside is an area of contradictory statistics. There is high unemployment – almost one in five people in the north of England is drawing unemployment benefit – yet there is a retail boom. The huge Metro Centre in Gateshead has been a commercial success from the moment its doors opened in 1986.

In Newcastle's Eldon Square shopping centre, 20 000 people an hour visited the 120 shops over Christmas 1986. They spent around £80m. Recently the managers of 90 big stores in the centre were asked about their trading prospects – 60 said they were either first or second in their company's national sales league.

Tyneside recognises the north–south divide as real. In terms of job losses, the 1984 Census of Employment made it easy to compare job losses in various parts of the country. The results are striking:

*Grainger Street in 1887*

Newcastle City Libraries

Job losses or gains:

| | 1979-86 | 1983-86 |
|---|---|---|
| Scotland | −172 000 ( 8%) | +12 000 (+1%) |
| North England | −138 000 (−10%) | +39 000 (+3%) |
| South East England | +172 000 (+2%) | +484 000 (+6%) |

Source: *Census of Employment 1984* and *The Guardian* 8 January 1987.

Even when the economy recovers, as it began to do between 1983 and 1986, the effects are felt more strongly in the South than in the North.

Newcastle upon Tyne was one of the main 'think-tanks' of the Industrial Revolution and, as a result, Tyneside was one of Britain's great bases of 19th-century industrial power. In common with Glasgow, Birmingham and Manchester, the area did not only make things – it made ideas as well. It was this aspect of Tyneside's past that Professor John Goddard of the University of Newcastle upon Tyne highlighted when asked to speculate about the future in the North East. At the University, Goddard is responsible for studying redevelopment and regeneration: he gives advice and help to cities and governments all over the world. The programme interviewers wanted to know what would happen on his own doorstep. Goddard pointed out that future success could not be based on the past tradition of heavy industry. But, he said, it could be based

*Neville Street and the Central Station in 1890*

Newcastle City Libraries

Newcastle City Libraries

*Quayside in 1880*

on the tradition of linking intellectual ideas with the practical world of products and services.

Goddard saw this partly as an intangible quality: the provinces had to take back from London and the South East some of the intellectual independence they had once had. But it was also a matter of creating the organisations and places where people could meet easily and so begin to work together. Tyneside shows several examples where this kind of development is taking place:

**The Innovation Centre**
This is a small complex of workshops in Gateshead where individual inventors or small businesses can obtain advice and help with product development. One of its aims is to make the local resources in higher education available to entrepreneurs. It seems to work particularly well in the electronics sector where a number of innovations have been successfully seen through from the original concept to pre-production prototypes.

### MARI (Microelectronics Applications Research Institute)

This organisation was set up in 1979 by Tyne and Wear County Council, Newcastle University, Newcastle Polytechnic and CAP, a commercial software company. There are a number of strands to MARI's activities, ranging from research projects to training courses for the computer specialists that Tyneside will need if it is to compete in the future. MARI is growing steadily and its operations are spreading beyond the Tyne. An interesting aspect of its economic role is that it is prompting the renovation and bringing back into use of a number of buildings of architectural quality that might otherwise have become derelict.

### Design Works

This is a project that is just beginning. With funds from the Urban Programme and the support of the District Council, the Burton Group is sponsoring the creation of a centre for design in Gateshead. The plan is to convert an empty Burton warehouse into studio, office and exhibition space. One motivation behind the scheme is the intention to encourage the North East's excellent design graduates to stay behind and help to create new products and services.

The Newcastle/Gateshead region is one of the places where the Government has set up a City Action Team (CAT) to co-ordinate funds coming from the three main departments responsible for inner-city regeneration. This team shares the vision of a centre of innovation and design on Tyneside and wants to help provide training facilities for the film and television industry and to add to the resources for market research and design. The CAT has recently helped to create an office and studio complex in the former stables of an old brewery near Newcastle city centre.

The environment where this development activity is taking place does not immediately suggest the typical range of urban problems.

Charles Mapleston

*Tyneside plans to remain in manufacturing, and one of the organisations that sets out to support this is an Innovation Centre where local inventors and business people can carry out the first stages of product development. This travelling car crusher is one of the products being developed at the Centre.*

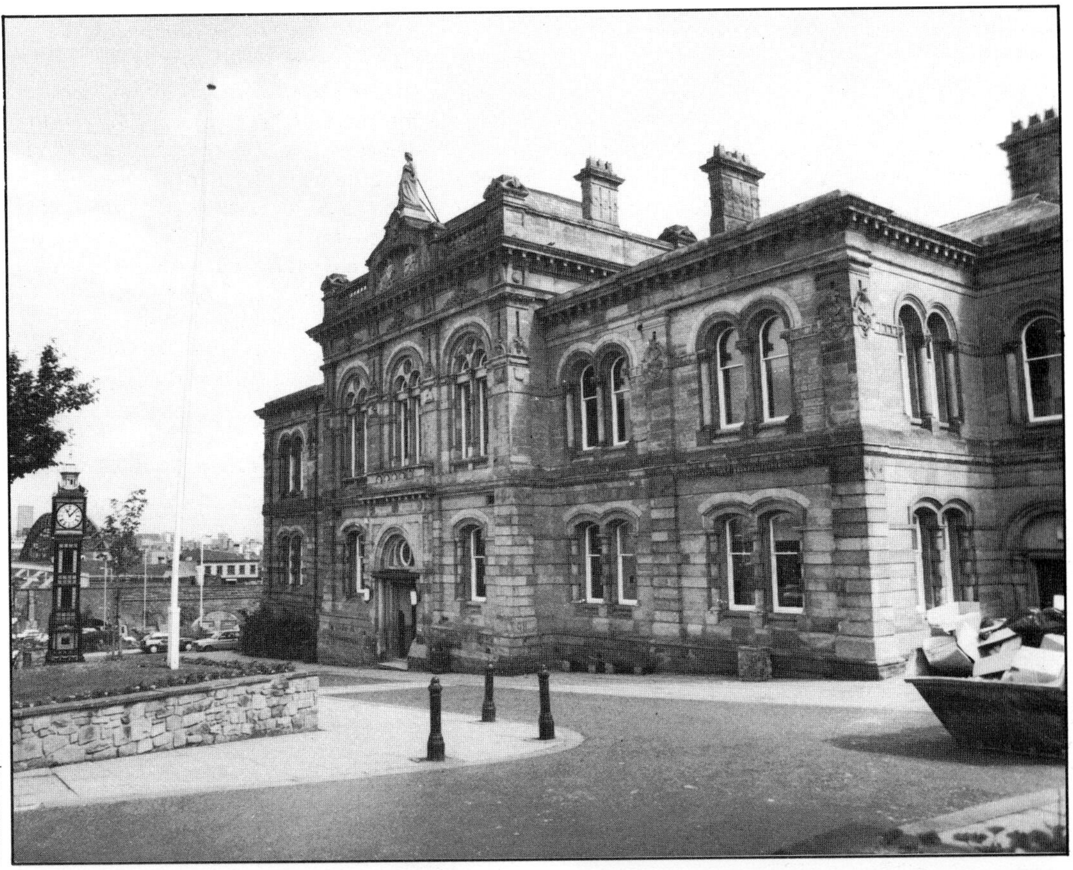

Charles Mapleston

*Gateshead's old Town Hall is one of the historic buildings used by MARI.*

Charles Mapleston

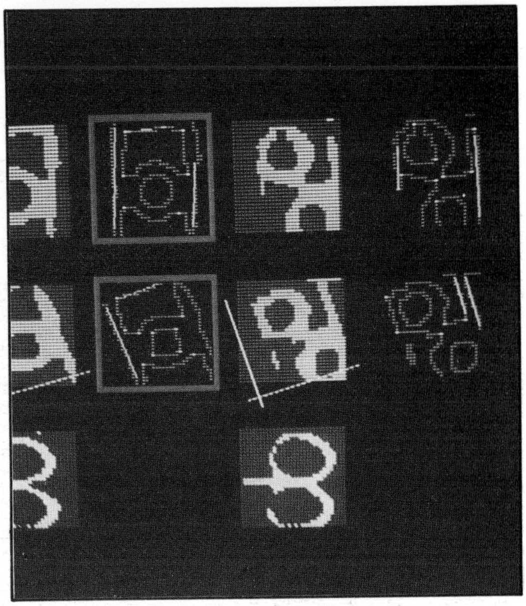

Charles Mapleston

*MARI is designing a robot sensor that will 'feel' and respond to the form of the things it is handling.*

A corner of Byker estate showing the private spaces and mature gardens.

Charles Mapleston

Helped by the staff of Newcastle Architecture Workshop, primary school children study Byker. The hope is that these future clients will recognise the importance of high standards of design.

Charles Mapleston

Newcastle developed at great speed in the 1960s and the city centre is prosperous and well kept. The Tyne and Wear Metro gives the area an excellent basis for its public transport system and the Metro Centre at Gateshead shows how strong the retail sector of Tyneside's economy really is. In Newcastle, the council is at last rescuing and refurbishing the historic buildings on the quayside, bringing life back to the site where Newcastle really began.

Behind this positive picture, however, there are large-scale environmental problems. There is derelict land along the Tyne where shipbuilding and engineering have declined. As in Glasgow, but on a smaller scale, many of the council flats and houses are in a state of disrepair, with some bordering on social collapse and abandonment. Bringing the Tyne back to life is a major environmental project and it may be difficult to achieve the right balance between housing, leisure and industry. The basic quality and potential of the river are splendid, and there are many good industrial buildings along its banks worth restoring. In terms of housing, the overall quality and international standing of Ralph Erskine's rebuilding of Byker provides a source of inspiration which local architects and tenants can follow successfully.

The vision of CAT is clearly of a city of modern technologists bordering the clean waters of the Tyne with attractive houses, factories, marinas and parks. To achieve this will mean establishing a firmer industrial base and alleviating the dire poverty of too many of the people who live there.

Charles Mapleston

*Newcastle has many poorly designed deck-access flats from the 1970s.*

Charles Mapleston

*In a recent scheme at Loadman Street these have been transformed by new planting, the creation of private spaces and good detailing. Here Newcastle Architecture Workshop worked with local people and the result is not only environmental improvement – new tenants' groups and social cohesion have emerged where before there was growing despair.*

# SOUTHAMPTON FACTS AND FIGURES

Population in the 1981 census was 209 800.

Southampton is, however, the main centre for a much larger area with a population of over 350 000, and the whole of southern Hampshire, from Southampton to Portsmouth and beyond, is rapidly becoming a continuous urban and suburban strip.

The population of the city itself is stable but that of the surrounding area is increasing.

Declining employment in the docks is crucial to understanding Southampton. Containerisation is one element, but Southampton has suffered, along with other British ports, from the change in emphasis from west to east coast ports. This is one effect of the growing importance Europe now has.

The percentage changes in trade for a selection of ports for the period 1970–80 are:

| | % |
|---|---|
| Felixstowe | +140 |
| Dover | +326 |
| Southampton | − 27 |
| Swansea | − 54 |
| Liverpool | −126 |

Southampton is one of the UK's six experimental free ports.

Although the docks themselves now employ many fewer dockers, the District Council estimates that 30 000 jobs in Southampton either depend directly on port activities or are there because the port is there.

*A photograph of fine docks taken during the strike of 1966. At this time Southampton was still the British base for the great passenger liners. A large part of this area next to the town centre is to be redeveloped as a series of marinas with shops, offices, restaurants and houses.*

Associated British Ports

'Here was a town that had not let the universal depression master it and that was contriving to enjoy its unique situation between forest and heath and deep blue water, a lovely bay window upon the world. It was not bad at all. Given a job to do and a bit of money in our pockets, you and I could live there and be reasonably happy. . . .'

This is what J B Priestley wrote about Southampton in 1934. He visited the town in the midst of what the historian, Adrian Rance, calls 'the golden era'. These were the days just after the completion of the new Western Docks, when the great ocean liners made Southampton their home. At the height of the docks' prosperity they employed 8000 men while the town's whole economy thrived on serving the ships, their freight and their passengers. Southampton stood out as an island of prosperity in the surrounding gloom of the Depression.

But the city had already experienced successive waves of prosperity and decline. Its position made sure that from a very early stage it would be an important mercantile and strategic town. Enclosed in a strong wall to keep out the French, medieval Southampton would have buzzed with trade and tradesmen. By then its shipping links had already spread far and wide – you would have heard many different languages being spoken in the streets.

On 15 August 1620 the *Mayflower* left Southampton for the New World, and after the turbulent period of the Civil War the town seemed to lose some of its importance. When Daniel Defoe visited it in 1723 he could write sadly of the decay of the 'once great port'. The next wave of development came from the sea but not from the harbour itself. In the 18th century the town became one of the new resorts that capitalised on the fashion for medicinal bathing and spa waters. The spa town era has left the modern city a legacy of good 18th-century buildings.

The Second World War created havoc: such an important port was a prime target for attack. Since 1945, it does not seem as though planners and architects have served the town well. The street plan became incoherent, with one or two tower blocks scattered incongruously among a higgledy-piggledy mixture of relatively small-scale old and new buildings. The new

*An advertisement for Southampton Docks, 1936.*

National Railway Museum

Southampton City Council

*The container port. The establishment of this modern and highly mechanised facility upstream on the River Test ensured Southampton's survival as a major cargo port but also released the old dock areas for development.*

*New houses at Ocean Village built on derelict dockland.*

Charles Mapleston

*The Altair, a superbly designed and made yacht that has recently been refitted at Shamrock Quay.*

Charles Mapleston

ocean liner terminal and a number of new shops were built in an insipid version of Festival of Britain 'modern'. The docks and the town began a very gradual process of decline that was masked at first by the prosperity of the country as a whole and the relative success of Southampton as a port.

Just as the docks had been the key to the golden era, so too they have emerged as the catalyst for the dramatic changes that are just beginning. Their tonnage has remained high but this tonnage depends on modern handling equipment which cannot be used in the older docks near the city centre. Employment in the docks has shrunk in a way that would have seemed impossible 20 years ago. In the 1960s the process of change was relatively slow and, as Alan Whitehead, Leader of the City Council, commented, 'the town was drifting along with no sense of direction'.

That now seems to have changed. There is agreement between the City Council, local developers, Associated British Ports and a number of entrepreneurs in the leisure industry that the future lies in a completely new approach. In one sense, what they are planning is a return to the values of the spa town. Southampton will use its excellent heritage of natural environment and historic building to earn its living. But to do this it has to use design to make the heritage visible, accessible and coherent.

Alan Whitehead summarises the strategy:

1 Open up the disused land in the docks to make it economically viable again. This will mean encouraging the building of houses, shops, offices and premises for small businesses. To achieve this will mean encouraging Associated British Ports to release as much derelict land as possible and encouraging developers to take the opportunity that this newly available land presents.
2 To make the city a boating capital for the South Coast. Many of the new developments in the docks will be related to boating, and the creation of attractive moorings with boatyard and leisure facilities is a first priority. The success of the approach can be seen in the private development at Shamrock Quay. This boating-based economy will provide a range

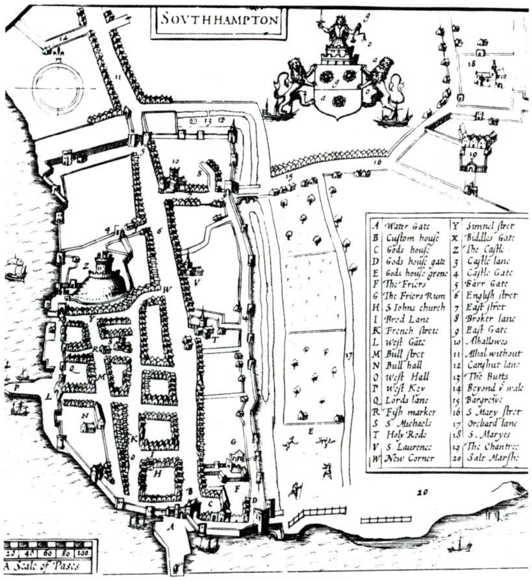


Southampton Planning and Development

Charles Mapleston

Southampton Planning and Development

*John Speed's map, drawn in 1611, shows the walls as they then were.*

*It is an essential part of Southampton's plan for the future to increase its tourist trade by emphasising its historical roots. A lovely Tudor garden has been designed and planted at one of the city's museums as a contribution to this idea.*

*A design for a bridge linking two parts of the existing walls. The District Council is working both to preserve the walls and create a walkway round them.*

of employment.

3 To make the town a centre for tourism. The aim here is to uncover and present all the elements in Southampton's historic past. This includes, for example, a major study of the town's splendid walls, and design and redevelopment work is under way to preserve them and make them accessible to the public as a city walk. In the same way, the council is encouraging private developers to refurbish old buildings rather than to demolish them. There are plans to create a visitor complex called 'Timebase' which will use all the expertise of the Yorvik approach to present history as an entertaining experience.

4 To improve the shopping environment and so to establish Southampton as a regional shopping centre.

5 To encourage the growth of new industries around the University.

# ADVICE, HELP AND TAKING ACTION

The United Kingdom is remarkable for the variety of its systems of government. England and Wales share a basic structure but Wales has its own distinctive cultural and development organisations: even the English regions are powerfully individualistic, many of them having created their own particular kinds of development agency on different occasions. Scotland has separate laws and institutions which are quite different to those south of the border. And in Northern Ireland the governmental status of the Province is so controversial that for the moment the major work of economic and environmental development has been taken from the local authorities to be administered by civil servants following guidelines laid down in Whitehall.

It follows that it is very difficult to give a general picture of who does what in regenerating industry and the environment, and who to go to if you want to take some action yourself. However, it is clear that the three ministries that have the greatest direct influence are the Department of the Environment, the Department of Trade and Industry and the Department of Employment. In Scotland and Wales government policy is implemented through the Scottish and Welsh Offices respectively: in Northern Ireland the Secretary of State operates from Stormont Castle using various government departments to carry out his policy.

It has been the Conservative Government's intention over the past decade to take a tighter grip on the policies and expenditure of local authorities and, as in London, to abolish the top tier of local government in the largest metropolitan areas in England. This has left the North East, for example, without a strategic planning authority, and the loss of the metropolitan county of Tyne and Wear is widely lamented on Tyneside. Some – but not all – look with a degree of envy on the Scottish and Welsh Development Agencies, seeing an effective means of achieving change in their large budgets and combined responsibility for industrial and environmental regeneration. Central government has now created new development corporations with similar powers for some English city areas but their budgets appear to be relatively small. In Northern Ireland, the Department of the Environment combines industrial and environmental regeneration in one organisation and there is a Secretary of State with special responsibility for Belfast.

In most areas of the United Kingdom, however, there are two levels of local government with a planning regeneration role: county or regional authorities and district councils. County or regional authorities usually have to take a broad view of developments over a wide area and this may involve holding the balance between towns with competing interests. By contrast, district councils are likely to represent local community interests. Both tiers can take initiatives, particularly in environmental regeneration. Frequently their funds are used for pump-priming, taking the risk to begin development in a new area where private investors have not yet been convinced of the eventual financial return. Often these ventures are very successful.

Increasingly, these local authorities are joining forces with one another, with central government, development agencies or finance houses in the private sector to launch new projects. Sometimes this is seen by them as welcome diversification, sometimes as ideologically unpalatable but, whatever the attitude, it is becoming the norm as cuts in local government expenditure bite deeper into local authority budgets. The fact is, even when they are short of funds, local authorities remain the greatest single influence on planning and development in the cities of the United Kingdom.

In recent years, central government has recognised something of the scale of the problem confronting inner cities and other areas of high unemployment. The Department of Employment, through the Manpower Services Commission, is responsible for encouraging new training which is required to cope with industrial upheaval; the Department of Trade and Industry is responsible for the 16 Inner City Initiative Taskforces, and provides support for manufacturers, including some interesting design support schemes; and the Department of the Environment is concerned with housing, roads and the rest of the physical infrastructure, with the exception of schools and hospitals. In attempting to help inner-city development the ministries have tended to work through a large number of local organisations ranging from established higher education bodies to new, self-help organisations that are much closer to the communities they serve. In some areas this diversity of action and funding receives careful co-ordination. On Tyneside, for example, a City Action Team is set up to make the most effective use of money from a variety of government sources in order to achieve success in a package of chosen developments.

There exists a large variety of financial inducements to manufacturers to locate their industry in areas of high unemployment, and unemployed people themselves can obtain government grants to help to set up their own small businesses. Developments in the fields of leisure and tourism are now beginning to attract similar support.

There has been a drastic cut in funds for local authority housing for rent. Some of these funds have been recycled to encourage the growth of independent providers of housing: for example, co-operatives and housing associations. In Scotland the Scottish Special Housing Association is particularly effective in providing well-maintained accommodation for rent. Co-operation between these bodies and district councils is now becoming an important feature of plans to regenerate cities in Great Britain, and in Ulster the Northern Ireland Housing Executive co-operates with them and with private builders.

In the following lists of sources of advice and help the aim is to include the addresses of those who produce useful publications or who have services available to the general public. However, for anyone with a specific problem or enquiry, it would be wise to go first to the local district council, all of which are now actively involved in economic regeneration as well as environmental development. From there the route of enquiry could follow different directions. It might go on to the local university or polytechnic which is running a 'technology transfer' scheme; it might be to contact the Design Council in London or one of its regional offices, or to go to a local innovation centre for help with product development; or it might be to go to see the co-ordinator responsible for facilitating local tenants' co-operatives.

However, local advice is not enough. One of the messages of the four programmes is: do not be parochial. Markets are now world wide. Many of our present ideas on city renewal have their origins in the United States. It is important to be aware of these wider horizons and to relate their promise to the local situation. Design is first and foremost about imagining the future, about speculating on what might be. Although ideas need to be capable of realisation, it is not helpful to be too constrained by narrow and established views. It is precisely that parochialism which has made UK industry so vulnerable to well-designed, forward-looking products designed and made in other parts of the world!

Parochialism is also a danger in another way. It is all too easy to see the answer to urban regeneration in just one design area, to go for excellent architecture or better product design, improved landscaping, or whatever. In fact, long-term success can only come from tackling all the design problems on a broad front: environmental design can improve people's living conditions and encourage local investment but, if the factories are making poor or out-of-date products that do not sell, the local economy will still fail to flourish and unemployment will continue to plague the area. Good product design by itself is not enough either: the entrepreneurs and investors necessary to exploit such products will not live or work in a run-down environment when they can easily take their talents to places that are more attractive.

## COMMUNITY ENTERPRISE

In July 1986 *The Times* and the Calouste Gulbenkian Foundation joined in the production of a compact guide to this developing area of activity. It includes a comprehensive address list. Copies can be obtained, free of charge, from:

Community Enterprise
Dept JDI, The Beacon Press
33 Cliffe High Street
Lewes
East Sussex BN7 2AN

Send an 18p stamped addressed envelope, size 229 x 164 mm. Charles Knevitt, the Editor, includes the following book list:

*The Phoenix Partnership: Urban Regeneration for the 21st Century,* by Harry Cowie. £4.00 inc p and p, from the National Council of Building Material Producers, 10 Great George Street, London SW1P 3AF.

Information Pack, free from The Shell Better Britain Campaign, Nature Conservancy Council, Northminster House, Peterborough PE1 1UA.

*Community Architecture: How people are creating their own environment,* by Nick Wates and Charles Knevitt. Published by Penguin (November 1987), price £3.95.

*Community Building Project Pack,* by Jane Stephenson and Jill Rawson. Free with a 50p stamped addressed envelope from the Urban Unit, National Council for Voluntary Organisations, 26 Bedford Square, London WC1B 3HU.

*Community Groups Handbooks,* by Jerry Smith and Maggie Pearce. Priced at £2.95 for a set of five handbooks, from the Community Projects Foundation, 60 Highbury Grove, London N5 2AG.

*Community Start-Up:* How to start a community group and keep it going, by Caroline Pinder. £4.95 inc p and p from the National Extension College, 18 Brooklands Avenue, Cambridge CB2 2HN.

*Business and the Inner Cities,* free with an 18p stamped addressed A4 envelope from Business in the Community, 227a City Road, London EC1V 1LX.

*Building Your Own: A Practical Guide to Planning Your Community Building.* Priced at £2.95 inc p and p, from the Scottish Community Education Council, Atholl House, 2 Canning Street, Edinburgh EH3 8EG.

A further, recent, information pack is *How to Start a Community Project* (£5.95 inc p+p), available from the Town and Country Planning Association, 17 Carlton House Terrace, London SW1Y 5AS.

A new bookshop has been opened, offering a world-wide mail order and distribution service for books and audiovisual material on all aspects of community architecture, planning, development and technical aid. It is:

Building Communities Bookshop
c/o T C Farries
Irongray Road
Lochside
Dumfries
Scotland DG2 OLH
Tel: (0387) 720755

A regularly updated, annotated catalogue is available on request.

One important type of agency in giving people design advice (either free or at low cost) is the community technical aid centre, of which there are one hundred throughout the UK. To find the nearest appropriate centre, contact the Association of Community Technical Aid Centres, The Royal Institution, Colquitt Street, Liverpool L1 4DE Tel: 051-708 7607.

A further source of help is Inner City Aid. The Inner City Trust was announced at the Building Communities Conference in November 1986. A registered charity, its purpose is to 'encourage and support self-help community development projects in deprived urban areas of the United Kingdom.' 'Deprived urban areas' is taken to include the outer estates.

Inner City Aid is located at:
8 Bedford Row
London WC1R 4BA
Tel: 01-430 0524 ext 145/126
Contact: Elizabeth Zub

## GOVERNMENT HELP

The main sources of help are the Department of the Environment, the Department of Employment and the Department of Trade and Industry. In England and Wales certain areas are eligible for help under specific environmental and training programmes. This is how the programmes were described in the Action for Cities campaign:

The Urban Programme is an important instrument of the Government's urban policy. It has promoted joint action by government departments, local authorities, the private sector and many local agencies which have a part to play in urban regeneration. Urban Programme assistance is now targeted on 57 localities, including most of the major cities. Within these areas projects are being packaged together so that they support each other.

The Action for Jobs campaign is also based on partnership between Government and the private sector. The Manpower Services Commission (MSC) makes the inner cities a priority in targeting its employment and training resources.

In 1985 the Government set up City Action Teams in London, Birmingham, Liverpool, Manchester/Salford, and Newcastle/Gateshead. The regional directors of government departments pool their efforts and together develop projects and programmes. Improved co-ordination and presentation leads to a more coherent involvement of the private sector.

The Government announced on 6 February 1986 a new initiative in the inner cities to improve the targeting and enhance the benefit to local people of the money channelled through existing central programmes. The initiative was originally mounted in 8 pilot areas; this was expanded to 16 on 27 April 1987. The contact names and addresses of the 16 pilot schemes are as follows:

**Coventry**
Derek Player
Rm 415, Copthall House
Station Square
Coventry CV1 2PP
Tel: (0203) 24310

**Hartlepool**
Brian Pollard
c/o Dept of Employment
Unemployment Benefit Office
21 Raby Road
Hartlepool
Cleveland TS24 8AX
Tel: (0429) 272227

**Nottingham**
Ian Samways
c/o Dept of Trade and Industry
Chalfont Drive
PO Box 2500
Nottingham NG8 3SS
Tel: (0602) 291111 ext 2645

**Doncaster**
David Wilkinson
c/o Doncaster Jobcentre
Queens Gate
Doncaster DN1 3LB
Tel: (0302) 215 71

**Birmingham**
Mark Tovey
227a Lozells Road
Handsworth
Birmingham B19 1RJ
Tel: 021-523 3241/6211

**Leeds (Chapeltown)**
John Lister
158-60 Chapeltown Road
Leeds LS7 4EE
Tel: (0532) 626 202

**Leicester (Highfields)**
Bob Fenley
3rd Floor, Horsefair House
3 Horsefair Street
Leicester LE1 5BP
Tel: (0533) 552248

**Middlesbrough (North Central)**
John Rundle
10th Floor, Corporation House
Albert Road
Middlesbrough
Cleveland TS1 2RU
Tel: (0642) 221162

**Bristol (St Pauls)**
Barry Cornish
FIND
189a Newfoundland Road
St Agnes
Bristol BS2 9NY
Tel: (0272) 550205

**Preston**
Howard Eastwood
8th Floor, Victoria House
Ormskirk Road
Preston PR1 2DX
Tel: (0772) 201770 ext 18

**Manchester (Moss Side)**
Pat Shilliday
7 Parisian Way
Moss Lane East
Moss Side
Manchester M15 5NQ
Tel: 061-226 8899/3375

**Rochdale**
Mike Clarke
Jobcentre
Octagon House
Yorkshire Street
Rochdale OL16 1BW
Tel: (0706) 523623

**Wolverhampton**
Fred Pickerill
50-54 Worcester Street
Wolverhampton WV2 4LL
Tel: (0902) 24005

**LONDON**

**North Kensington**
Colin Francis
2 Acklam Road
London W10 5QZ
Tel: 01-960 8455

**North Peckham**
Daniel Levy
2nd Floor, 72 Rye Lane
Peckham
London SE15 5DQ
Tel: 01-358 9018/9019/9020

**Tower Hamlets**
Ian Rosser
3rd Floor, Cityside House
40 Adler Street
London E1 1EW
Tel: 01-377 1866

The objective of the inner cities initiative is to increase the effectiveness of central government programmes in meeting the needs of communities in urban areas suffering from especially severe problems – in particular through improving their employment prospects and encouraging enterprise.

Development opportunities must be taken up and derelict areas cleared to stimulate the confidence needed for investment. Equally important is the need to improve training skills. People need help to be able to compete for the new jobs. Enterprise must be encouraged and cities need new businesses to replace those that have declined.

The Government has supported and developed a wide range of programmes aimed at training and enterprise, and at helping development.

**Supporting training and enterprise**
Youth Training Scheme
Community Programme
Restart Programme
Local Enterprise Agencies
Small Firms Advice
Enterprise Allowance Scheme
Adult Training

**Helping development**
Urban programme
Urban Development Grant
Urban Regeneration Grant
Urban Development Corporations
Derelict Land Grant
Land Registers
Enterprise Zones
Simplified Planning Zones
Estate Action

Here are addresses to contact for more information:

**Nationally**
Department of Environment
Inner Cities Directorate
P2/119, 2 Marsham Street
London SW1P 3EB
Tel: 01-212 0492/5240

Department of Employment
Inner Cities Central Unit

5th Floor, Caxton House
Tothill Street
London SW1H 9NF
Tel: 01-213 5588/4666

Department of Trade and Industry
Information Division
1 Victoria Street
London SW1H OET
Tel: 01-215 4465

Manpower Services Commission
TMS2 Inner Cities Division
Moorfoot
Sheffield S1 4PQ
Tel: (0742) 704198/704288

**Or Locally**
London City Action Team
The Regional Director
Greater London Regional Office
Department of the Environment
Room 2516, Millbank Tower
21-24 Millbank
London SW1P 4QU
Tel: 01-211 5419

Birmingham City Action Team
The Regional Director
West Midlands Regional Office
Department of Trade and Industry
Ladywood House
Stephenson Street
Birmingham B2 4DT
Tel: 021-632 4111 ext 581

Liverpool City Action Team
The Director
Merseyside Task Force
Room 404, Graeme House
Derby Square
Liverpool L2 7SU
Tel: 051-227 411 ext 580

Manchester/Salford City Action Team
The Regional Director
North West Regional Office
Department of Trade and Industry
Room 822, Sunley Tower
Piccadilly Plaza
Manchester M1 4BA
Tel: 061-2171 ext 664

Newcastle/Gateshead City Action Team
The Regional Director
MSC Northern Region
Broadacre House
Market Street
Newcastle upon Tyne NE1 6HH
Tel: 091-232 6181 ext 224

The Regional Director
Yorkshire and Humberside Regional Office
Department of the Environment
Room 1062, City House
New Station Street
Leeds LS1 4JO
Tel: (0532) 438232 ext 2236

The Regional Director
South West Regional Office
Department of the Environment
Tollgate House
Houlton Street
Bristol BS2 9DJ
Tel: (0272) 218811 ext 8490

The Regional Director
East Midlands Regional Office
Department of the Environment
Cranbrook House
Cranbrook Street
Nottingham NG1 1EB
Tel: (0602) 476121 ext 311

The Regional Director
Manpower Services Commission
The Pithay
Bristol BS1 1UR
Tel: (0272) 273710

The Regional Director
Manpower Services Commission
2nd Floor, Maid Marion House
56 Houndsgate
Nottingham NG1 6BH
Tel: (0602) 410088

The Regional Director
Manpower Services Commission
Jubilee House
33-41 Park Place
Leeds LS1 2RJ
Tel: (0532) 446299

In a similar way the Department of Trade and Industry directs help to certain specific areas. For further information on these specific areas, contact the following regional offices of the Department of Trade and Industry:

**North East**
Department of Trade and Industry
Stanegate House
2 Groat Market
Newcastle upon Tyne NE1 1YN
Tel: (0632) 324722

**North West**
Department of Trade and Industry
Sunley Buildings
Piccadilly Plaza
Manchester M1 4BA
Tel: 061-236 2171
and
Department of Trade and Industry
(Liverpool Office)
Graeme House
Derby Square
Liverpool L2 7UP
Tel: 051-227 4111

**Yorkshire and Humberside**
Department of Trade and Industry
Priestley House
Park Row
Leeds LS1 5LF
Tel: (0532) 443171

**East Midlands**
Department of Trade and Industry
Severns House
20 Middle Pavement
Nottingham NG1 7DW
Tel: (0602) 506181

**South East**
Department of Trade and Industry
Ebury Bridge House
2-18 Ebury Bridge Road
London SW1Q 8QD
Tel: 01-730 7235

**West Midlands**
Department of Trade and Industry
Ladywood House
Stephenson Street
Birmingham B2 4DT
Tel: 021-632 4111

**South West**
Department of Trade and Industry
The Pithay
Bristol BS1 2PB
Tel: (0272) 272666
and

Department of Trade and Industry
South West Industrial Development Office
Phoenix House
Notte Street
Plymouth
Devon PL1 2HF
Tel: (0752) 21891

**Scotland**
Industry Department for Scotland
Alhambra House
45 Waterloo Street
Glasgow G2 6AT
Tel: 041-248 2855

**Wales**
Welsh Office Industry Department
Government Buildings
Cathays Park
Cardiff CF1 3NQ
Tel: (0222) 825111

Welsh Office Industry Department
North Wales District Office
Government Buildings
Dinerth Road
Colwyn Bay
Clwyd LL28 4UL
Tel: (0492) 44261

**Northern Ireland**
Industrial Development Board for Northern Ireland
IDB House
64 Chichester Street
Belfast BT1 4JX
Tel: (0232) 233233

## ADVICE ON PRODUCT DESIGN

### The Design Council

The Design Council was set up by the Government in 1944 as an independent, but Government-sponsored, organisation to promote by all practicable means the improvement of design in the products of British industry. The Council's remit covers industrial and engineering design and it is funded by a grant from the Department of Trade and Industry, with further revenue earned from the sale of publications, from the Design Centre shops, and other services.

Policy is approved and its implementation monitored by a Council of 25 members appointed by the Secretary of State for Trade and Industry. The Design Council is a registered charity and is incorporated by Royal Charter.

A new initiative to put design to work by giving expert advice on product development to selected companies in three areas of Britain has recently been announced by John Butcher, Under Secretary of State for Trade and Industry. Services available from the Design Council are listed below:

The Design Advisory Service
Support for Design Scheme
Designer Directory
Marketing Services
The Design Protection Advisory Service
Design Centre Selection
Design Centre Shops
Teaching and Learning Resources
Publications
British Design Awards.

To find out more, or apply for a supported design study, write to or telephone:

The Design Council
28 Haymarket
London SW1Y 4SU
Tel: 01-839 8000
Telex: 8812963

**Midlands and the North**
The Design Council
Norwich Union House
31 Waterloo Road
Wolverhampton WV1 4BP
Tel: (0902) 773631

**North West**
The Design Council
Sunley Buildings
Piccadilly Plaza
Manchester M1 4EA
Tel: 061-228 2593

**Scotland**
The Design Council Scotland
The Scottish Design Centre
72 St Vincent Street
Glasgow G2 5TN
Tel: 041-221 6121

**Wales**
Y Cyngor Cynllunio
The Design Council Wales
Pearl Assurance House
Greyfriars Road
Cardiff CF1 3JN
Tel: (0222) 395811

**Northern Ireland**
The Design Council Northern Ireland
Windsor House
9-15 Bedford Street
Belfast BT2 7EG
Tel: (0232) 238452

## The Crafts Council

The Crafts Council is a government-funded body to support the crafts in England and Wales and to promote the work of artists/craftspeople.

For further information, write or telephone:

The Crafts Council
12 Waterloo Place
London SW1Y 4AU
Tel: 01-930 4811

## ADVICE ON ENVIRONMENTAL DESIGN

The Royal Town Planning Institute
26 Portland Place
London W1N 4BI
Contact: Tony Fyson

The Landscape Institute
12 Carlton House Terrace
London SW1Y 5AS
Tel: 01-839 4044

The Town and Country Planning Association
17 Carlton House Terrace
London SW1Y 5AS
Tel: 01-930 8903

The Civic Trust
17 Carlton House Terrace
London SW1Y 5AS
Tel: 01-930 0914

The Royal Institute of British Architects
66 Portland Place
London W1N 4AD
Tel: 01-580 5533

## The Royal Institute of British Architects

The Royal Institute of British Architects (RIBA), founded in 1834, aims to extend knowledge of architecture and the role of architects, and to maintain standards in the profession and in architectural education. Approximately 27 000 architects form the membership of the RIBA.

*Community Architecture*

One way in which the RIBA has become involved in the regeneration of both urban and rural areas is through community architecture. Its aim is to improve the quality of the environment by involving people in the design and management of the buildings or space they occupy.

The RIBA also runs a community architecture Resource Centre at its London headquarters, which provides information on community architecture projects and initiatives. Enquiries are welcome by telephone, by letter or in person. The Centre can also provide the name of the local community architecture regional co-ordinator, who can advise on getting a project started. *The Times*/RIBA Community Enterprise Scheme makes annual awards, to encourage community initiatives where local enthusiasm and drive has been advanced with the support and assistance of community architects and other professionals.

For further information about community architecture, contact
Stella Yarrow
Community Architecture Secretary
66 Portland Place
London W1N 4AD
Tel: 01-580 5533 ext 4033

*RIBA Regional Offices*

*Scotland*
Royal Incorporation of Architects in Scotland
Secretary:
Charles McKean
15 Rutland Square
Edinburgh EH1 2BE
Tel: 031-229 7205

*Wales*
Society of Architects in Wales
Executive Secretary:
Richard Fairlamb
Midland Bank Chambers
75a Llandennis Road
Rhydypennau
Cardiff CF2 6EE
Tel: (0222) 762215

*Ulster*
Royal Society of Ulster Architects
Secretary:
Frances McMorris MBE
23 Mount Charles
Belfast BT7 1NZ
Tel: (0232) 223760

## NORTHERN IRELAND, SCOTLAND AND WALES

The following are sources of help that have special responsibility for industrial or environmental development:

### Northern Ireland

Department of the Environment for Northern Ireland
Urban Affairs Branch
Parliament Buildings
Stormont
Belfast BT4 3ZZ
Tel: (0232) 63210 ext 2355

Industrial Development Board for Northern Ireland
IDB House
64 Chichester Street
Belfast BT1 4JX
Tel: (0232) 233233

Local Enterprise Development Unit
LEDU House
Upper Galwally
Belfast BT8 4TB
Tel: (0232) 691031

### Scotland

Industry Department for Scotland
Alhambra House
45 Waterloo Street
Glasgow G2 6AT
Tel: 041-248 2855

The Scottish Development Agency
120 Bothwell Street
Glasgow G2 7JP
Tel: 041-248 2700

### Wales

Industry Department for Wales
Cathays Park
Cardiff CF1 3NQ
Tel: (0222) 825111

The Welsh Development Agency
Pearl Assurance House
Greyfriars Road
Cardiff CF1 3XX
Tel: (0222) 222666